ZEN TEACHING,
ZEN PRACTICE

Philip Kapleau and
The Three Pillars of Zen

ZEN TEACHING, ZEN PRACTICE

edited by Kenneth Kraft

New York · WEATHERHILL · *Tokyo*

First Edition, 2000

Published by Weatherhill, Inc.
41 Monroe Turnpike, Trumbull, CT 06611

Library of Congress Cataloging-in-Publication Data

Zen teaching, Zen practice: Philip Kapleau and the Three pillars of Zen
edited by Kenneth Kraft
     p.   cm.
   ISBN 0-8348-0440-9
    1. Kapleau, Philip, 1912– 2. Spiritual life—Zen Buddhism.
    I. Kraft, Kenneth, 1949– II. Three pillars of Zen
BQ968.A863 Z46 2000
294.3'927'092—dc21

Contents

EDITOR'S NOTE: To avoid excessive notes, citations from *The Three Pillars of Zen* are not annotated. Diacritical marks on all non-English words have been removed.

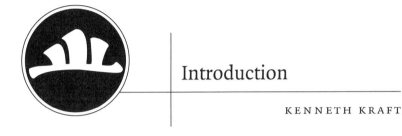

Introduction

KENNETH KRAFT

The Three Pillars of Zen: Teaching, Practice, and Enlightenment, published in 1965, was the first book by a Westerner writing from within the Zen tradition. The author-editor, Philip Kapleau, was a former court reporter who had left his work to undergo twelve years of Zen training in Japan. Zen was already recognized in the United States and Europe through the writings of Japanese experts and Western enthusiasts, but little was known about Zen *practice*. The book came to the attention of a small group studying Asian thought in Rochester, New York, and their support enabled Kapleau to found the Rochester Zen Center in 1966. Then a spiritual tidal wave hit. Interest in Asian religions swelled, and *The Three Pillars of Zen* became a bible for the first generation of American Zen practitioners. It has remained in print in English,[1] and has been translated into ten languages: Chinese, Dutch, French, German, Italian, Polish, Portugese, Spanish, Swedish, and Vietnamese. One of these, Chinese, is the original language of Zen.

The creation of such an influential book would have been accomplishment enough, but the author proceeded to "walk his talk." When hundreds of people, most of them in their twenties, flocked to the Zen

8

Center, Kapleau stepped into a role that was unprecedented in the West. He became a Zen teacher to a large community, and built a flourishing organization with affiliate groups in North America, Mexico, and Europe. For twenty-five years he regularly conducted intensive meditation retreats (*sesshin*), the heart of the rigorous style of training that he favored. His subsequent books addressed a wide range of topics from a Buddhist perspective.[2] Kapleau retired as abbot of the Zen Center in 1986, but continued to teach and write. Eventually he sanctioned seven senior disciples, four men and three women, as spiritual heirs qualified to guide students on their own.[3] At the age of eighty-seven his physical health is frail, but his warm personal manner and sense of humor are undiminished.

When *The Three Pillars of Zen* was published, the available Western-language books on Zen took up only a few inches of shelf space. Most of them presented the subject in abstract terms, extoling rarefied modes of consciousness but giving little indication how people had gone about achieving such states. *The Three Pillars of Zen* was the first book to emphasize the role of seated meditation, or *zazen*. Illustrations showed six correct meditation postures, from the cross-legged full-lotus position to sitting in a chair. Further information on Zen practice was presented in lectures and commentaries by Kapleau's two principal teachers. In a section called "Eight Contemporary Enlightenment Experiences of Japanese and Westerners," eight practitioners described personal odysseys that culminated in their attainment of *kensho*, the Zen term for an initial experience of enlightenment. One of the accounts, by "Mr. P. K., an American ex-businessman," was Kapleau's own story.

This material conveyed a new and startling message: that ordinary people could follow the way of Zen and experience its fruits for themselves. Through an unanticipated alchemy, a Western "ex-businessman" elucidating a monastic Asian discipline seemed to be speaking directly to a budding generation of spiritual searchers. Not only was Kapleau's voice recognizable, it seemed at times as if it were one's own voice. His words rang true. Some readers wondered how far this unusual book could take them. Might it even hold the key to enlightenment itself?

Kapleau's portrayal of Zen became the first model of Zen practice for many Westerners. Whatever their reactions to that model, many readers found that Kapleau's presentation maintained a tenacious hold on their understanding of Zen—those initial impressions were not easily revised.

The Three Pillars of Zen has accordingly served as a benchmark against which other Zen books have been measured. Only a few have achieved comparable stature, most notably Shunryu Suzuki's *Zen Mind, Beginner's Mind*, published in 1970. *The Three Pillars of Zen* not only inspired many people to undertake Zen practice themselves; it also opened the door to Buddhist thought and spirituality for countless non-Buddhist readers.

As an author, Kapleau is by turns a cool-headed reporter, a resolute seeker, and an ardent ambassador of Zen. He divulges his own yearnings and missteps in diary extracts from the earliest days of his training. Religious writers perennially try to express the sensation of being caught between the persistent pain of life and the promise, however faint, of liberation. Kapleau says it this way:

> I'm still the hungry dog next to the tank of boiling fat that is satori:
> I can't taste it and I can't leave it.

At one point, after a peak of exertion in the meditation hall, he fainted. (For a beginner, anything that dramatic feels like a sign of progress.) His teacher, Harada Roshi, helped to carry him to his room:

> Roshi anxiously peers into my face, asks: "You all right, you want a doctor?" . . . "No, I'm all right I guess." . . . "This ever happen to you before?" . . . "No, never." . . . "I congratulate you!" . . . "Why, have I got satori?" . . . "No, but I congratulate you just the same." . . . Roshi brings me a jug of tea, I drink five cups.

In a passage composed years after these diary entries, he writes in a different voice about the relation between zazen meditation and enlightenment:

> In the long history of Zen, thousands upon thousands have attained enlightenment through zazen, while few genuine enlightenment experiences have taken place without it.

Others might qualify such statements, but Kapleau does not waver. The book also includes fluent translations of classic Zen texts, produced in collaboration with Japanese colleagues. Kapleau knew how to write before he found Zen. Marshaling his talents in the service of his biggest assignment, he created a work that was both a summation of a religious tradition and an intimate spiritual autobiography.

KRAFT

Philip Kapleau was born on August 20, 1912, in New Haven, the fifth of six children. Both parents were immigrants. His father was Eastern Orthodox Christian, and his mother Jewish, though neither was especially religious. In high school Kapleau formed an Atheists Club—until the threat of expulsion forced him to disband it. "We could never imagine what Philip would think up next," one of his older sisters later recalled. "He was a mystery to us."[4] Kapleau graduated from high school during the Depression, and he never had the opportunity to attend college. Instead, he learned shorthand, took courses at night school, and pursued a career in court reporting.

He was working as a court reporter at the Tokyo War Crimes Trials in 1947 when he first encountered Zen. When the trials were over, he returned to the United States and tried his hand at business, but he soon became deeply dissatisfied with the life he was leading. At a loss what to do next, he recalled the peace he had felt when he visited Buddhist temples. So in 1953 he went back to Japan, this time to seek out Zen.

An introduction to a Zen master who spoke some English led to further introductions, and within a few months Kapleau attended his first meditation retreat, an unexpectedly powerful and transforming experience. Soon afterward he was accepted as a "lay monk" at Hosshinji, an active Zen monastery in rural north-central Japan. The Zen teacher (*roshi*) at Hosshinji was Harada Sogaku (1870–1961), eighty-four and full of energy. For almost three years Kapleau immersed himself in monastic life. In October of 1956 he wrote in his diary:

> In just two months three years will have elapsed since I first came to Hosshin-ji.... So much water has flowed under the stone bridge, or should I say so many stone bridges have flowed over the motionless water?... Have toiled with the monks in the heat of summer and shivered with them on snowy *takuhatsu* [gathering alms], felled trees, planted rice, cultivated the gardens, cleaned the outhouses, and worked in the kitchen with them. I've shared their heroic, dedicated moments, joined in their petty intrigues....
>
> Sitting, sitting, sitting, one painful sesshin after another, then more zazen morning after morning, night after night, and night into morning.... Dazzling insights and alluring visions have filed through my mind, but true illumination, satori, still eludes me.

Introduction

That fall Kapleau left Hosshinji, moved to Kamakura (near Tokyo), and continued to practice fervently as a layman under Yasutani Hakuun Roshi (1885–1973), one of Harada Roshi's sanctioned heirs. Time and again he presented himself before his teacher in *dokusan*, the private master-student encounter vital to certain modes of Zen training. Two more years passed, and then, during a hot August *sesshin*, Kapleau sensed that he was close to some kind of breakthrough. As the energy mounted, he again approached his teacher:

> Hawklike, the roshi scrutinized me as I entered his room, walked toward him, prostrated myself, and sat before him with my mind alert and exhilarated…. "The universe is One," he began, each word tearing into my mind like a bullet. "The moon of Truth—" All at once the roshi, the room, every single thing disappeared in a dazzling stream of illumination and I felt myself bathed in a delicious, unspeakable delight…. For a fleeting eternity I was alone—I alone was…. Then the roshi swam into view. Our eyes met and flowed into each other, and we burst out laughing.

Four days later Kapleau wrote, "Feel free as a fish swimming in an ocean of cool, clear water after being stuck in a tank of glue…and so grateful."

Kapleau practiced under Yasutani's guidance for seven more years, eventually receiving Yasutani's permission to teach Zen. During this time he continued to work on a project conceived during his early days at Hosshinji: a book on Zen for Westerners by someone who had undergone actual training. As the manuscript neared completion, something else seemed to be ending as well—he realized it was time to go home.

When I first met Philip Kapleau, in February, 1970, he was energetically introducing Americans to Zen, not only in Rochester but also in many other parts of the country. I was twenty, a junior at Harvard, exploring. I registered for an off-campus workshop on Zen conducted by someone whose name, surprisingly, was not Asian. When Kapleau demonstrated the full-lotus posture, it was the first time I had seen a living person sit in meditation, and the sight struck me with great force. So calm! So stable! Clearly this was a very different way of using the body and the mind, unlike anything I had been taught. In that posture, Kapleau wordlessly offered an alternative source of authority—experiential, religious, ancient—at a time when so many other forms of authority were being discredited. In the ensuing years he became both

KRAFT

teacher and honored friend. Though I am calling him Kapleau here, ordinarily I call him Roshi. And while a retrospective assessment requires the past tense, he is still fully present.

Those who are unfamiliar with Zen practice are sometimes surprised to learn of the importance of the teacher. In Zen, a teacher is someone further along on the path (ideally, much further along) who can inspire and guide others. From an institutional standpoint, certification to teach is obtained after completion of a prescribed course of training and study. From a spiritual standpoint, a teacher is supposed to have attained enlightenment, at least to some degree.[5] In English, the term "Zen master" has come to be used somewhat indiscriminately, in part because there are so few alternatives, whereas Japanese offers half a dozen terms from which to choose, depending on the teacher's stature. An effective Zen teacher can function as a tireless coach, a stern critic, a fierce general, or a nurturing parent, without getting stuck in any of those roles. He or she must also serve as a repository of the tradition, its lore as well as its wisdom. Because Zen teaching is about how to live, it has no fixed content or form. A master may be teaching when he says, "Good morning."

Singer Joan Baez once remarked, "All of us are looking for the guru. And at the same time you know *the* guru has to be a phony."[6] Most Zen students would agree. In contrast to some other religious traditions, a Zen teacher is not an infallible authority or an object of devotion. However skilled, he or she cannot bestow enlightenment. Rather, the teacher strives to guide the student—in any way possible—so that the student's own exertions stay on track. Since the ultimate teacher is reality itself, a Zen teacher's job is described as "selling water by a river." This reluctance to put teachers on pedestals also serves as a check on the teachers (most of whom continue to struggle with the wiles of ego). As a psychologist has observed, "If you are a Buddhist meditation master, it is infinitely more difficult to proclaim yourself permanent authority and sole arbiter of legitimacy, because there lies behind you, as ballast, 2,500 years of corrective teaching."[7]

When I visualize Roshi Kapleau at the height of his teaching career, I see him seated imposingly in a cross-legged posture in the room where he conducted the private encounters called dokusan. During an intensive meditation retreat he would see as many as sixty students two or three times a day. Usually he did not say much, but watched and listened intently, head slightly cocked, dark-brown eyes alive. A raised eyebrow or a clearing of the throat were not good signs, and a frown meant trouble, but when an involuntary half-smile played across his lips it was immeasurably encouraging. When he spoke, it sometimes felt as though he was speaking from inside oneself. As a teacher, Kapleau was demanding, unshakably centered, and seemingly indefatigable. Besides administering a large (and in the early days, turbulent) Zen center, he took on hundreds of insistent students in an intensely personal way. Zen training brings many dark moments when one questions the validity of Buddhist teachings and doubts the real chances of self-transformation. At such times a teacher fulfills his most important function of all, offering living proof that the Buddha Way can indeed be realized.

Kapleau's modest build, gentle demeanor, and slightly hoarse voice belied his strength and versatility. He was an unusual kind of intellectual, undaunted by a lack of academic credentials, emboldened by Zen's traditional disapproval of mere book-learning. As a writer, he was quietly proud of the success of his books. He could not quite give up working on a book even after it was published; several were revised and even retitled in subsequent editions. He was an abbot of rare foresight who also paid close attention to the color of an altar cloth or the pattern of a walkway under construction. Other personae were less public: amateur collector of Buddhist art, devotee of traditional Japanese cedar bathtubs, lifelong harmonica player.

Kapleau often had difficulty explaining to others what had impelled him at the age of forty-one to abandon an apparently normal life and seek such an arduous and alien alternative. In 1979 he reflected:

> It seemed at times that what had motivated me to surrender my middle-class comforts and values to undergo Zen training was the desire to find relief from painful tensions and an exhausting restlessness. At other times I felt it was a need to understand the appalling sufferings I had witnessed in Germany, Japan, and China just after World War II. Eventually I realized that the answers to the foregoing questions lay in one word—karma, a term embracing the whole concatenation of causes and effects that is one's life.[8]

One could analyze Kapleau's life and work in psychological or social terms, taking into consideration his family background, emotional needs, and patterns of behavior. Perhaps a childhood and adolescence in near-poverty molded his formidable will or made him singularly receptive to the prospect of "rapid upward spiritual mobility."[9] But that approach, however edifying, would still miss the mark. When Harvard psychiatrist Robert Coles contemplated the life of Dietrich Bonhoeffer, the Christian theologian martyred during World War II, he concluded that conventional yardsticks fail to take the measure of deeply religious or deeply spiritual people, who sojourn in a dimension that transcends history and culture. According to Coles,

> We were, really, trying to comprehend a life fueled by spiritual ener-gy through a way of thinking that had little to do with religious ideals as they get turned, by some, into intensely guiding principles: [we were] secular minds unable to fathom the workings ... of a mind tied significantly to the sacred.[10]

The Three Pillars of Zen is in large measure a book about *kensho*. An early section offers the following explanation of kensho, in the words of Kapleau's teacher Yasutani Roshi:

> It is the sudden realization that "I have been complete and perfect from the very beginning. How wonderful, how miraculous!" If it is true kensho, its substance will always be the same for whoever expe-riences it, whether he be the Buddha Shakyamuni, the Buddha Amida, or any one of you gathered in this temple. But this does not mean that we can all experience kensho to the same degree, for in the clarity, the depth, and the completeness of the experience there are great differences.

The Japanese word kensho (*chien-hsing* in Chinese) is composed of the two ideographs "see" and "nature." The usual English rendering is "to see one's true nature." The term has its origins in the classic texts of Chinese Zen (Ch'an), including the last line of the four-line stanza that traditionally defines Zen: "see [one's true] nature and become a bud-dha" (Jp., *kensho jobutsu*).[11] Among English speakers, the better-known equivalents of kensho are enlightenment and satori. In *The Three Pillars of Zen* these three terms are used more or less interchangeably, with one qualification:

> In describing the enlightenment of the Buddha and the Patriarchs,

however, it is customary to use the word *satori* rather than kensho, the term satori implying a deeper experience.

In the more than three decades since the publication of *The Three Pillars of Zen*, the notion of kensho—and, more broadly, the idea of enlightenment—has been challenged in various ways. Some of the questions have arisen within Zen communities. Meditators who looked forward to kensho as an existential Big Bang that would change their lives forever were dismayed and perplexed when that did not happen. For some, *The Three Pillars of Zen* was itself a source of inflated expectations. The discrepancy between anticipatory visions of enlightenment and actual experiences of insight is a recurring theme in the essays assembled here.

Further doubts arose when senior practitioners behaved badly, and especially when recognized Zen teachers violated basic moral standards. If such people had achieved kensho and could nonetheless act unethically, something was askew—either they were not as enlightened as they were supposed to be, or enlightenment itself was overrated. Recently, studies of World War II–era Japan have unearthed another problem: most of the leading Zen masters, including the teachers prominent in *The Three Pillars of Zen*, embraced the rampant nationalism and militarism of imperial Japan. Again, a doubt: Wouldn't an enlightened master see through such misguided passions?

Scholars have raised questions of a different nature. Zen's valuation of individual experience as a touchstone of authenticity troubles those who view experience as conditioned and indeterminate. Zen language is a source of concern for others. Because Zen texts exhibit a "rhetoric of immediacy" and adhere to a "rule of rhetorical purity," what those texts describe may be suspect.[12] Another school of thought holds that many aspects of Zen practice, such as the master-student encounter and formal meditation, have a ritual dimension that is often overlooked. For one scholar, the ubiquity of ritual extends even to enlightenment:

> Zen "enlightenment," far from being a transcultural and transhistorical subjective experience, is constituted in elaborately choreographed and eminently public ritual performances.[13]

Seasoned Zen students acknowledge that many of these challenges to traditional claims about kensho and enlightenment express a truth—up to a point. Kapleau himself, in his later teaching, offered two clarifica-

KRAFT

tions. First, he reiterated that there are varying degrees of depth, just as there are various ways to wake up from (ordinary) sleep:

> In ordinary awakening one may barely open one's eyes, half asleep in a twilight zone, or one may open one's eyes fully and jump out of bed. With *kensho*, seeing into one's nature, one may see dimly or with great clarity; the gradations are many and subtle.[14]

Second, he drew a sharper distinction between the words kensho and satori. Kensho is defined specifically as "a first awakening, usually shallow," whereas satori is reserved for "spiritual awakening that brings about a fundamental transformation of personality and character and a wholly fresh vision of the world."[15]

The authors in this book do not hesitate to enter the fray. Is kensho best understood as an experience, a state of mind, a form of knowledge, a mode of activity, all of those, or none of them? And what is the relation between a particular moment of insight and a way of life consonant with such insight? Since most of the contributors have been deeply involved in Zen for twenty-five or more years, they are able to compare their present understanding of kensho with their former conceptions and misconceptions. Thomas Merton once wrote, "Let us remember that the contemplative life is first of all *life*, and life implies openness, growth, development."[16] In that same spirit, it is possible to affirm kensho while recognizing its "no-thingness," to substantiate it without substantializing it. Bodhin Kjolhede, in the concluding essay, calls this "standing by enlightenment without resting in it."

Just a few years before the publication of *The Three Pillars of Zen*, a respected scholar observed, "Whether the spokesmen of Buddhism admit it or not, Buddhism is not yet a live option in the religious life of people outside Asia."[17] When Kapleau started setting up the Rochester Zen Center, no one was certain what lay ahead. Buddhism has since become a "live option" outside Asia, and Zen appears to have taken root in the West. Our lack of surprise is itself an indication of the distance that has been traversed. Albert Stunkard, in the opening essay, recalls a time and place—Kamakura, Japan, 1947—that surely marks one point of departure. When Zen scholar D. T. Suzuki tried to tell two young

Americans, Stunkard and Kapleau, about the delights of "satori," only a handful of Westerners had ever heard the word ("and I was not one of them," Stunkard adds).

The teachers who have disseminated the aims and methods of Buddhist practice in the West have participated in a turning point in the history of Buddhism. Future historians of religion may one day look back on this period as "a first propagation." What began as a rough-and-tumble experiment by a small number of people developed into a multifaceted movement that continues to find points of entry into mainstream society. Where would one look to see if Zen has indeed been transmitted to the West? The durability of Zen centers, the proliferation of Zen books, the signs of Zen influence in art and culture, the growth of Zen studies in academia—all of these merit consideration. *Zen Teaching, Zen Practice* proposes another source of evidence, perhaps most important of all: the lives of individuals who have embraced Zen practice. In less than forty years, many practitioner communities (Sanghas) have witnessed the maturation of a first generation, the ascent of a second generation, and even the debut of a third.

During his years of training in Japan, Kapleau anticipated that an American Zen would have its own distinctive character, and this belief grew stronger when he began teaching in the United States. "I felt that the worst accusation you could make against a religion was to call it foreign," he has said.[18] Though we are too close to the indigenization of Zen in the West to define "American Zen" with certainty or precision, a rough outline would probably include the following points: insistence on texts in English, independence from the authority of Asian progenitors, incorporation of psychological perspectives, openness to social engagement, and gender equality. Two elements deserve special consideration: awakening, and its availability to laypeople as well as monastics. The encounter of Buddhist spirituality and Western egalitarianism may lead to a democratization of enlightenment.[19] Taken negatively, that phrase could imply a watering down of wisdom or the selection of roshis by referendum. Taken positively (my preference), it can signify the actualization of Zen practice in secular settings and "ordinary" lives. In that sense, the democratization of enlightenment is a good working definition for American Zen, provided the authenticity of insight is maintained. For Kapleau, this is familiar territory—with an unerring sense of direction, he planted his banner on this very spot.

Thoughtful people can often look back to a particular book that unveiled a new world and may even have set their life on a different course. In *Walden*, Thoreau wrote, "How many a man has dated a new era in his life from the reading of a book!"[20] *The Three Pillars of Zen* had this effect on most of the contributing authors, so I invited them to use it as a springboard for their reflections. Adept commentary should also be able to stand on its own. One can enter these essays directly, whether or not one is familiar with *The Three Pillars of Zen*.

The contributors include three of Roshi Kapleau's sanctioned heirs, now teachers themselves: Bodhin Kjolhede has been abbot of the Rochester Zen Center since 1986; Sunyana Graef has been the teacher at the Vermont Zen Center for over a decade; and Mitra Bishop recently inaugurated Mountain Gate Zen Center outside Santa Fe. Other senior disciples of Kapleau demonstrate the viability of lay practice in various walks of life: Wes Borden is a professor of chemistry, Casey Frank a lawyer, and Rafe Martin a writer and storyteller. Victoria Kieburtz, a doctor, was introduced to Zen by Kapleau but has done most of her training with Kjolhede. Representatives of other lines of American Zen corroborate Kapleau's wider influence: Arnold Kotler is a teacher in Thich Nhat Hanh's order, and Alan Senauke was ordained as a Zen priest by Sojun Mel Weitsman. Josh Schrei is the grown son of former staff members at the Rochester Zen Center, and psychiatry professor Albert Stunkard befriended Kapleau half a century ago in postwar Japan.

In Zen lore the legendary monk Bodhidharma is honored as the first person to have brought Zen teachings from India to China, early in the sixth century. He exemplifies the old Buddhist adage that "the Buddha's teachings flow ever eastward." The climax of Bodhidharma's journey was his crossing of the Yangtze River on a single reed. There are classic Zen paintings of the Indian monk balanced serenely on his reed like a virtuoso waterskier, his tattered robe catching the wind. This image, a visual metaphor for transcendence, also allows a touch of irony—after all, what is there to transmit that is not already present in abundance? Buddhism made a historic leap eastward in the latter half of the twentieth century through the efforts of bold-spirited pioneers. Philip Kapleau is prominent among them, and so is his mode of conveyance, *The Three Pillars of Zen*, which has proved to be a good reed as well as a good read. I imagine that Bodhidharma would be pleased.

Introduction

ZEN TEACHING,
ZEN PRACTICE

I | Philip Kapleau's
First Encounter with Zen

ALBERT STUNKARD

Philip Kapleau and I were both introduced to Zen Buddhism early in 1947. We were in Japan with the postwar American Occupation. I was working in Tokyo as an army medical officer at Sugamo Prison, providing medical care for the men who were being tried for war crimes by the International Military Tribunal for the Far East. Phil was working as a court reporter at the Tribunal. Our introduction to Zen came at the hands of Dr. D. T. Suzuki, a distinguished Zen scholar and a leading figure in Zen's transmission to the West.

One of the prisoners, later to become recognized as a religious thinker, was Graf Duerckheim, a German. He used to talk to me about Zen. One day he mentioned Dr. Suzuki, with whom he had studied, suggesting that I visit Dr. Suzuki at his home in a small town not far from Tokyo.

I took up the suggestion and not long afterwards met Dr. Suzuki in his house on the grounds of Engakuji monastery in Kita Kamakura. He was standing in his garden, a small, bald man in a brown kimono, pruning shears in hand. He looked up from his work and came forward, with a quizzical look and a warm smile. Dr. Suzuki welcomed me, took the letter of introduction from Graf Duerckheim, and led me inside his house, where he adjusted his spectacles and read the letter. I had a chance to look at him more closely. He was slender and a bit frail, with a face dominated by huge eyebrows that curved upwards and outwards.

When he had finished the letter, Dr. Suzuki asked me about Duerckheim and the other prisoners at Sugamo. He said that he was pleased to learn that I was interested in Zen, and invited me to return the following Sunday afternoon when he would be free. Even during this brief encounter, I sensed the man's serenity.

When I returned on Sunday, Dr. Suzuki began to speak about Zen and, soon, about "*satori*." At the time, only a few Westerners were familiar with the term, and I was not one of them. "Satori is the alpha and omega of Zen Buddhism," he declared. "Without satori, there is no Zen Buddhism." But what was this satori? From what I could gather, it seemed to be some kind of profound experience in which "body and mind fell off." Dr. Suzuki took pains to explain that the experience was not psychological. Rather, he called it "noetic," not a concept that meant a lot to me. Someone who underwent this experience was transformed, he said, and no longer saw the world as divided into subject and object. How such a person did see the world was beyond words.

In that faraway time and place, all of this sounded very strange. But, coming from this smiling little man, it was also intriguing. I called Ted van Itallie, an old friend who was then serving as a medical officer at the United States naval base at Yokosuka, not far from Kita Kamakura. I told him about Dr. Suzuki and asked him if he would join me to see what he thought of all this. The next Sunday afternoon, Ted and I listened closely to Dr. Suzuki as he talked about Zen and this mysterious satori with its incredible fruits. Afterwards, as we walked out of the monastery grounds in silence, I waited for Ted's reaction. When it did not come, I prompted him. Recalling our psychiatry course in medical school, I said, "It sounds like schizophrenia, doesn't it?" Still there was no reply. "What do you make of it?" I insisted. Ted waited a while longer, and then he said, "Well, even if it *is* schizophrenia, I'll buy it."

Ted van Itallie's visit was just the first of many wonderful Sunday afternoons at Engakuji, as other young Westerners joined the discussions in Dr. Suzuki's house. The next person to come was Dick DeMartino, who had gone to the military's Japanese-language school in Boulder, Colorado, and so had an enviable command of Japanese. He

Philip Kapleau's First Encounter with Zen

used this skill as an investigator for the defense of the Japanese prisoners who were being tried for war crimes before the International Military Tribunal. Dick's job was to roam over the country looking for any evidence that could be used to help the defendants at the trial. Since these were the same men for whom I was caring at Sugamo Prison, our paths sometimes crossed. Shortly after Dick joined the Sunday afternoon sessions, he brought his friend Philip Kapleau, whom he had met in the course of his duties.

In this way, the International Military Tribunal brought the three of us together. Dick and I were removed from the actual courtroom events, one of us learning about the past deeds of the main characters, the other caring for their current ills. But Phil the reporter had a ringside seat to watch the drama as it unfolded. At the time, the trial was seen by some people as a major step forward in international law and the regulation of human affairs. However, for others it was nothing more than a victor's justice meted out to the vanquished. Whatever the trial's ethical implications, it was high drama. As the terrible events of the war were reviewed, the actors played their parts in the shadow of the gallows. The imminence of death was inescapable, and it affected those of us who knew the accused men in one way or another. This was the atmosphere in which some of us began to explore Zen.

The next person to join our group was Richard Crewdson, a young Englishman who had survived four years in the elite Grenadier Guards. During the war all of the other officers in his company had been killed or seriously wounded. He too was concerned with death.

Occasionally we were joined by two fascinating men. One was the poet R. H. Blyth, who had spent the war years as an enemy alien in Japanese prison camps. He eschewed the chairs that the rest of us were only too happy to use and would sit quietly on his knees, listening to Dr. Suzuki with evident awe. The other occasional visitor was Faubion Bower, a distinguished Japanese scholar who had served as an interpreter for General MacArthur during the war. Bower knew a great deal more about Zen and Dr. Suzuki than we did. He approached the sessions from the perspective of a culture historian rather than as a seeker of Buddhist wisdom.

When we arrived at the quaint little semi-rural railroad station at Kita Kamakura, we first crossed to the other side of the tracks. Then we walked up ancient stone steps worn smooth over the years, flanked by huge dark cryptomeria trees. We passed under Engakuji's massive "mountain gate" with its thatched roof, then came to a fence that enclosed Dr. Suzuki's small house and garden, partially hidden by foliage. For many of us, this was our first chance to see the inside of a Japanese house. In war-ravaged Tokyo there was not a wooden house left standing. The only structures that rose above the ground were tall, thin chimney-like "go-downs," which had been used to store valuables and other household materials.

Dr. Suzuki's modest wooden house had straw tatami mats for the floor and sliding paper-covered doors for the walls of the rooms. In a bright area near glass doors, facing the garden, was a low desk with a typewriter on it. Often we would arrive to find Dr. Suzuki seated on a cushion on the floor, hunched over his typewriter. He wore a green eyeshade when he wrote.

The Sunday afternoons began with a cup of tea. Sometimes it was Japanese green tea poured from a pitcher into small white cups. If there were only two or three guests, Dr. Suzuki would produce large irregular glazed bowls. He prepared the tea one bowl at a time, first by ladling green tea powder with a bamboo spoon. Then he poured hot water into the bowl, beat the tea into foam with a little whisk, and served it. Quietly, unpretentiously, he was showing us the tea ceremony.

After tea, we would settle down and talk. Often we visitors began with questions that had occurred during the past week or had been stimulated by our reading. Dr. Suzuki's responses were encouraging yet often enigmatic. Sometimes he spoke about theory, such as the subject-object dichotomy and the overcoming of that dichotomy in satori. Sometimes he told how people in the past had "obtained" satori. He was fond of the story of the monk who, after years of seeking, was transformed when he heard the click of a stone raked against a bamboo tree. Occasionally one of us would comment or attempt to interpret what Dr. Suzuki had been saying, even about satori. At this point he would nod, smile benignly, and say, "Very good. Not quite, but very good."

These afternoons led us to a preoccupation with satori and how it might be obtained. It seemed so highly desirable, so transforming, to the point of overshadowing any other concerns. Dr. Suzuki managed to create an impression, even an expectation, that the lightning of satori might strike at any moment. He spoke about being alert and aware all of the time. However, as the months passed, we began to feel that our kind of alertness and awareness was not going to be enough.

Philip Kapleau's First Encounter with Zen

Dr. Suzuki rarely mentioned *zazen*, the actual practice of Zen meditation. I later learned that this was a period in his life when he believed that zazen was not necessary to understand Zen. The Westerners in our little group, tantalized by the wonders of enlightenment but not knowing how to get there, felt increasingly frustrated. At times I would think irreverently that Dr. Suzuki was like a doctor who diagnosed a fatal disease and then told the patient that there was no treatment for it. Yet something about the man himself kept us returning Sunday after Sunday.

When our various tours of duty in Japan came to an end, we returned home. To our surprise, Dr. Suzuki followed us. He had accepted an invitation to give a series of lectures at Columbia University. At least four members of our Engakuji group began to attend his lectures: Van Itallie, Kapleau, DeMartino, and me. The lectures were very similar to the old Sunday afternoon conversations with this remarkable man, transplanted from his monastery home to a New York City classroom. There was the old talk about satori and how Chinese monks in the T'ang dynasty had attained great spiritual heights, but again no concrete advice as to how to follow in their footsteps.

Some of the attendees at Dr. Suzuki's lectures were more than satisfied with an intellectual appreciation of Zen and Asian culture. Others lost interest and drifted away. But for Philip Kapleau, a real tension had arisen between the promise of enlightenment and the agony of his daily life. In *The Three Pillars of Zen*, writing as "Mr. P. K., an American ex-businessman," he describes his anguish:

> April 20, 1953: Attended S____'s [Suzuki's] Zen lecture today. As usual, could make little sense out of it.... Why do I go on with these lectures? Can I ever get satori listening to philosophic explanations of *prajna* [wisdom] and *karuna* [compassion] and why A isn't A and all the rest of that? What the hell is satori anyway? Even after four of S____'s books and dozens of his lectures, still don't know. I must be awfully stupid.... But I know this: Zen philosophy isn't ridding me of my pain or restlessness or that damn "nothing" feeling.

Among the people who attended the Columbia lectures, a number eventually took up Zen practice. Yet Kapleau did not wait to take action: he quit his business, sold his belongings, and moved to Japan. There he encountered three masters whose presentation of Zen was not at all like Dr. Suzuki's.

It has become fashionable to think of D. T. Suzuki's extensive writings on Zen as unbalanced and misleading, especially in regard to satori. I have sometimes shared this view. But then I wonder if a more sober, warts-and-all account of Zen would have aroused the same degree of interest among Westerners. Would it have baited the trap as effectively? Would Philip Kapleau have had to go back to Japan to resolve the questions that gripped him? I think not. In Zen, deep spiritual questioning is called the "great doubt." An axiom of practice is: the greater the doubt, the greater the enlightenment. Without really intending it, Dr. Suzuki raised the great doubt in Philip Kapleau.

Fifty years later, I remember these events with great affection.

2 | Tall Branches, Tender Leaves

WES BORDEN

.

Thirty years ago I read *The Three Pillars of Zen*, and it changed my life. *The Three Pillars* was the first book to go beyond the purely philosophical Zen found in the writings of D. T. Suzuki and Alan Watts, and to establish the connection between *zazen* (Zen meditation) and *kensho* (first awakening). The development of Zen practice in the West owes much to the genius of Philip Kapleau in incorporating into *The Three Pillars* the enlightenment accounts of laypeople, including his own story, with vivid descriptions of the efforts that led these people to kensho. The effect of the book on me and countless others was to motivate us to get off our chairs and onto meditation cushions, out of our thoughts about enlightenment and into our bellies, to begin to concentrate our minds. If being inspired by *The Three Pillars* to practice zazen is what many Western Zen students have in common, what makes each of us unique is the particular chain of events that resulted in the book's effect on us, and the manner in which Zen training has subsequently transformed our lives.

At the time that Philip Kapleau was making his first trip to Japan, to attend the war crimes trials, I was growing up in New York City. In 1951, when I was eight, my parents moved to an affluent suburb so that my younger sister and I could attend the excellent public schools there. I was loved by my parents; we were financially well off; and I felt secure. But, starting when I was about ten years old, that changed.

Around 1953 my father lost the company job he had held for many years. Although he soon found a comparable position, within a few months he had lost that job too. I did not connect what was to become a cycle of his getting and losing jobs with his hospitalization for some sort of mental illness when we lived in New York City, but the connection became apparent when I was twelve. In 1955 my father had been unemployed for a long period. From the many changes in my family's lifestyle, I sensed that my parents' savings were almost depleted. However, just before Christmas that year my father was hired by a large company for an executive position better than any that he had previously held. Our financial worries seemed at an end, and I was tremendously relieved. I assumed that the feeling of security would last forever.

Forever lasted two months. I came home from a friend's birthday party one Saturday night to find my father packing his suitcase. He explained that his company had asked him to do something that he thought was very wrong and that, rather than do it, he was now going to buy the company and run it himself. Since I knew that the company was very big, to me that sounded crazy. When my father left, I asked my mother what was going on. She explained that my father suffered from manic-depressive illness and was now in a manic phase. She was sure that he had already been fired. My poor mother! As I parent, I can now see how hard it must have been for her to share this information with me, especially since in the mid-1950s matters as serious as the mental illness of a parent were usually kept from children.

I began to sob and could not stop. I sobbed so hard that I threw up several times. Blood vessels in my eyelids broke, and my eyelids turned purple. I cried because I loved my father so much, yet I was helpless to prevent what was happening to him. I sobbed because I sensed (correctly, as it turned out) that his pattern of being hired, becoming manic, and then getting fired was going to be an endless cycle. But most of all I cried because that night I had lost the innocence of my youth—the confidence that nothing really bad could happen to me and my family, the belief that everything would always end happily. I can only imagine how much my mother, seeing my extreme reaction, must have regretted her candor.

Tall Branches, Tender Leaves

Four years later my great aunt, who was like a grandmother to me, unexpectedly died while she was staying at our house. She was fine when I went out after dinner, but when I returned at 11 P.M., she was dead. A few months after that my mother finally succumbed to the lung cancer she had been fighting for several years. The following year my mother's best friend, who had helped my sister and me survive my father's manic-depressive illness after my mother's death, committed suicide. However, these three losses seemed less painful than the loss I suffered at age twelve, when I realized that happy endings are by no means guaranteed.

Interestingly, soon after this realization I was sitting under a tree in our yard on a warm spring day when I suddenly had the sense that there was something very important that I was supposed to do with my life, although I did not have a clue what it was. Three years later a girl slightly older than me, and with whom I was infatuated, gave me Hermann Hesse's *Siddhartha* to read. The book provided the first inkling of what it was that I was supposed to do, wanted to do, with my life. I wanted to get enlightened, but only after having lots of interesting experiences, like Siddhartha in Hesse's novel. Over the next several years this young woman served as my mentor, giving me some of Alan Watts's books to read and, subsequently, telling me about the experiments that Timothy Leary and Richard Alpert were doing at Harvard with psychedelic drugs.

By this time I was myself an undergraduate at Harvard. Although I was majoring in physics and chemistry, I took a course in social psychology. The subject that intrigued me most was how one's membership in a socio-linguistic community filters and alters the way one experiences the world. What struck me was that neither the instructor nor any of the assigned readings seemed to consider the question, How is it possible to experience reality directly, without its being distorted by this filter? Psychedelic drugs were being touted by Leary and Alpert as allowing one to do just this, and I wrote a term paper on the subject, for which I interviewed Leary. I also began experimenting with psychedelic drugs on my own. However, I soon became convinced that, although psychedelic drugs might temporarily open the door to a different type of perception and cognition, I was not going to get enlightened by ingesting chemicals.

After college, I spent a year in Cambridge, England. Cambridge University had a very active Buddhist organization, and I attended a lecture each week and went to meditation sessions each Sunday, led by a former monk from Thailand. I also started reading books on Theravada Buddhism. The lecturer who had the greatest impact on me was a Canadian monk who had spent a number of years in Southeast Asia doing Vipassana meditation. I attended a meditation retreat at his center in Scotland, but I found Vipassana meditation to be too passive for me. I was seeking instant enlightenment—an attitude that stemmed from my own impatient nature and my experience with psychedelic drugs. Nevertheless, Vipassana was better than anything that I had yet found. For the next several years I tried to meditate for half an hour every morning, and I did solitary retreats on weekends and for a week or two every summer.

On my return to the States, some friends introduced me to Louise March, a teacher in the Gurdjieff work. Mr. Gurdjieff was an early-twentieth-century mystic of obscure origins, who taught first in Russia and then in Europe and the United States. I liked Mrs. March instantly, probably because she reminded me of my great aunt. Both were powerful women who minced no words and did not suffer fools gladly. Mrs. March had been Gurdjieff's personal secretary, and I felt that she embodied some of the qualities of Gurdjieff himself.

I guessed that Mrs. March liked me too, because she went out of her way to give me a hard time. As she once put it, "I did not stick pins in you; on you I used knitting needles." For example, soon after I met her, she turned to me and said, "You are a giraffe. You go from tree to tree, eating only the tenderest leaves on the topmost branches," and she proceeded to perform a credible imitation of a giraffe fastidiously doing just that.

During my stay at the farm that Mrs. March and her students had bought in upstate New York, I found that I also had the ability to be a sewer rat. The amount of human waste produced by the large number of people living there had overwhelmed the farm's septic system, and I was assigned to the crew that was extending the old sewer line. On my first day I found myself standing in a muddy field, looking down into a water-filled trench from which the unmistakable smell of human excrement wafted. I can remember praying that none of the waste had leached into the mud in which I stood. However, after a few days of work, I had completely forgotten my revulsion. I stood knee-deep in the trench, groping with my fingers in the muck at the bottom, trying to feel for the stones that interfered with the slope of the pipe we were laying. When Mrs. March returned from a brief trip, she found me covered

Tall Branches, Tender Leaves

with shit. She took one look and exclaimed, "Ha! Now you are much more essential."

ROSHI PHILIP KAPLEAU   In 1969, I was living in Boston, attending Gurdjieff group meetings, doing Vipassana meditation, and practicing aikido every morning at a *dojo* (training hall). That summer I happened to read *The Three Pillars of Zen*. For the first time in my life I really felt that there was a practice—the practice of zazen described in the book—that could enable me to find what I was seeking. I did not know what "enlightenment" was, but I knew that I wanted to get enlightened myself. As soon as I learned about the Rochester Zen Center, I signed up for a workshop there.

My first impression of Roshi Kapleau was hardly that of the dynamic Zen master I had expected. (He was then called Sensei, which means teacher.) I saw a slight, middle-aged man whose manner, especially the way he stopped in mid-sentence to search for a word, reminded me of a slightly absent-minded college professor. However, two things he said made a deep impression on me. Someone asked, "Is an enlightened person enlightened about everything?" Roshi Kapleau replied, "To imagine that enlightenment brings an instant understanding of history, economics, politics, or anything like that is foolish. In Japan I met many spiritually developed people whose opinions on such subjects I would not have trusted." Remembering this statement over the past thirty years has stood me in good stead. It saved me from "roshi worship"—the belief that one's Zen teacher has great wisdom on any and every subject—and the disillusionment that follows when one discovers that roshis too have areas of great ignorance, even about themselves.

Someone else was brave enough to ask, "What is enlightenment?" Roshi Kapleau removed his watch and said, "Normally we just see the front of the watch, but there is a backside too. Unless we have seen both the front and the back, we really don't understand what a watch is, do we? We live in the world of relativity, but unless we have also seen the world of the absolute, we don't really understand what life is. Enlightenment is seeing both sides simultaneously." My first reaction to this comparison of seeing a watch to enlightenment was to think, "How corny! How can this teacher hope to attract students by saying something so simple-minded about something so profound?" But then I thought, "Maybe he isn't trying to attract students, and maybe for him enlightenment is as simple and ordinary as a watch."

BORDEN

After the formal end of the workshop, participants who were interested in becoming members of the Zen Center were invited to meet with Roshi Kapleau privately. When I entered the interview room, the person whom I encountered was not the person I had seen all day at the workshop. Roshi Kapleau was kneeling in the posture that the Japanese call *seiza*, his back erect, his face impassive yet serene. The visual impression was striking, but even more powerful was the sense that this person was totally present in a way I had not previously experienced in anyone else. In that moment I knew that I had found the teacher I had been seeking. In the thirty years that have passed since then, I have never once thought otherwise.

Unfortunately, although I was certain that I had found my teacher, he seemed equally certain that he did not want me to be his student. My application to join the Rochester Zen Center was summarily rejected. In the rejection letter, Roshi wrote, "Since you are already involved in Gurdjieff work, Vipassana, and aikido, you cannot make a serious commitment to Zen." I immediately wrote back that I was willing to give up all these other activities to practice Zen. So I was accepted as a member, and in 1970 I returned to Rochester to attend my first *sesshin* (meditation retreat).

I was determined to get a koan, a Zen problem that defies the intellect, and use it to get enlightened at that very sesshin. Early in the morning of the first day, with great anticipation and excitement, I went to my first *dokusan* (private meeting with the teacher). When I entered the dokusan room, I found the same presence I had encountered in the interview after the workshop. To my urgent request that he give me a koan, Roshi responded calmly and almost kindly that I should begin by counting my breaths. Deflated, I returned to the *zendo* (meditation hall). As the morning rounds of zazen continued, I first grew bored, and then I began to wish that I had never come to sesshin. I was sleepy. I could not concentrate. My legs began to ache. I was hit with the *kyosaku* (encouragement stick), and it really hurt. As the first day progressed, I began to get scared.

I was scared especially by the steadily increasing pain in my legs, worried that the pain might become so intolerable I would have to break the strict rule about not changing one's posture during a round of zazen. When I tried surreptitiously to move a knee or an ankle a few inches, to help relieve the pain, I found myself in an even more uncomfortable position. There seemed no way to escape the pain. Nor could I escape the blows of the kyosaku—I seemed to get hit when I least expected it.

Tall Branches, Tender Leaves

I also believed that no one else in the zendo was having the same difficulties I was experiencing. Many of the others were sitting beautifully in the full-lotus posture on a single cushion. I was kneeling in a modified form of seiza, with innumerable cushions of different shapes and sizes piled under me in an effort to keep as much weight as possible off my feet and ankles. I was sure that I was the worst sitter in the zendo and that everyone else was going to get enlightened long before me. In fact, if this was really the path to enlightenment, I was *never* going to get enlightened, because I hated zazen and I hated sesshin. I had no desire ever to do either again. Surely there must be some easier way to get enlightened, but I did not know of any. I felt trapped.

Between rounds of zazen I hid in my bed, trying to sleep. However, even if I slept, the zendo was still there waiting for me when I awoke. I counted the days until the end of sesshin. In the zendo I spent more time counting the minutes until the end of each round than I spent counting my breath. "Two minutes left? Certainly not five. Oh God, don't let it be more than five. If it's more than five I'll have to move. Come on, ring the bell to end the round. *Please* ring it!"

And still I did not have a koan, so I felt that all this physical and mental suffering was in vain. Each time I went to dokusan I asked Roshi for a koan, and each time he said, "Keep counting your breath, and by the end of sesshin you will have a koan." I thought, "The *end* of sesshin? That's too late." Finally, on the afternoon of the third day, Roshi apparently lost patience with me and exclaimed, "You are a spiritual butterfly, flitting from flower to flower. Someone with your attitude cannot get through a koan, so it would be irresponsible of me to give you one." I burst into tears and shouted back at him, "That's not true! Give me a koan, and I will show you!" Roshi replied, "Alright, at your next dokusan I will give you a koan."

At my next dokusan I reminded Roshi that he had promised to give me a koan. He said, "I will give you Joshu's Mu to work on, but only if you are absolutely sure that you can get through it." By this time, all the confidence that I had expressed in my previous dokusan had evaporated, but I lied and said, "I can get through Mu." Roshi briefly presented the koan, a dialogue in which a monk asks if a dog has buddha nature. Its kernel is Zen master Joshu's enigmatic answer "Mu," which literally means no. Then, apparently as an afterthought, Roshi added, "By the way, I notice that you are sitting in seiza all the time. At least for some rounds, can't you sit in a better posture?" "Yes," I volunteered. "I can sit in quarter-lotus, but only for short periods." (The quarter-lotus is a cross-legged posture, with one foot placed on the calf of the other leg.) "Good," said Roshi. "Try alternating rounds of quarter-lotus with seiza." Before I could explain that by "short periods" I meant fifteen minutes at most, he rang his handbell, ending the interview.

Now I really was in deep trouble, because a round of zazen lasted thirty-five minutes. However, if I didn't sit in quarter-lotus, what would Roshi think of me, especially after I had told him how determined I was to get through Mu? I had no choice but to start sitting in quarter-lotus. The second half of each round that I sat in quarter-lotus was sheer agony. I was sure that I would be permanently crippled. I found that the only way to get through those last fifteen minutes was to concentrate unremittingly on Mu and to put Mu in my knee, in my ankle, or wherever the pain was worst. If I did that, the pain did not go away, but it became bearable. However, if my attention flagged and I began to think about the end of the round, the pain came back with full force. So I stopped allowing my thoughts to wander—whenever a thought arose, I blew it away with Mu.

"Just Mu. Only Mu. Mu. Muu. Muuu." Despite the fact that it was midwinter in Rochester, and the zendo was unheated, I ended each round that I sat in quarter-lotus soaked in sweat. My cushions grew soggier and soggier as my concentration grew stronger and stronger. I had hold of Mu now, and I was determined to break through it. It felt like a huge rock; and I thought that if only I pushed hard enough, it would topple over. I put all my energy into my *hara* (lower belly) and began physically to push with it as hard as I could. "Muuu. Muuuu. Muuuuuuu."

Suddenly, darkness gave way to light, and I wondered if I had gotten kensho. At my next dokusan I asked Roshi to test me. After he had listened to my responses to several questions, he said, "If you really had gotten through Mu, you would have answered those questions very differently. However, your concentration is deepening. Try pushing less with your body and boring in more with your mind."

I returned to the zendo and did my best. My hatred for sesshin fueled my work on Mu. I was determined to get through Mu this sesshin and never come back to another. Of course, I did not tell Roshi Kapleau that, not until many years later. He laughed and said, "I was the same way, and my teacher, Harada Roshi, knew it. Before each sesshin he would say, 'Kapleau-san, if you can get through Mu at this sesshin I will

buy you a ticket back to America.' But my desire to escape from sesshin
did not get me through Mu."

Nor did mine, not in my first sesshin or in any of the others that I attended during the ensuing five years. Sometimes Mu was strong, and I became elated. Often, during the very next round of zazen, Mu became so weak that I dreaded having to go to dokusan. Slowly I learned to stop judging my practice and just to do my best. Experience taught me that whatever the state of my practice at a given point, it would change, often several times, during the course of a day and throughout the sesshin. I also began to learn to do what Roshi had suggested, to push less with my body and to concentrate more intensely with my mind. I found that if I pushed too hard with my body, my breathing became too tight, and the energy rose from my hara into my chest. Rather than pushing against Mu, I tried to become one with it; my Mu became like the cry of a lover calling out to his lost love.

Sometimes, when Mu was strong, Roshi would suddenly shoot a test question at me, such as "What is the color of Mu?" If he liked my answer, he might ask a second: "Where do you see Mu?" Once, something very strange happened in dokusan. Roshi asked me a test question, and without a flicker of thought or an instant of hesitation, the answer burst forth. For days afterward, I puzzled over who had answered that question, for it certainly was not "I."

At my first sesshin, I had been desperate to get through Mu. In subsequent sesshins, although I certainly still wanted to get through Mu, getting through the sesshin became even more important. I lied to myself about how important getting through Mu was to me, but I never quite abandoned myself to this task as totally as I had during my first sesshin. In my heart of hearts, I did not really believe that I could get through Mu; had I been more honest with myself, I might have stopped going to sesshin altogether.

Roshi Kapleau has said that if we cannot motivate ourselves to practice seriously, events in our lives often supply the motivation for us. This is exactly what happened to me, five years after I started practicing Zen. At that point, I was a professor of chemistry at the University of Washington in Seattle, and my wife was pregnant with our first child. I was giving a lecture at a university on the East Coast when I received an emergency phone call from my mother-in-law. She said that my wife, who suffered from a severely curved spine, had started having such intense muscle spasms in her back that her doctor was afraid she might lose the baby. Because of the pregnancy, the doctor did not want to give my wife any pain medication or muscle relaxants; he could do nothing but let her suffer. And suffer she did. I returned home on the first available flight and found her lying in bed in dreadful pain, unable to move. When she had to urinate, I placed a towel between her legs to soak up as much urine as possible, but there was little else that I could do to make her more comfortable.

To see the person whom I most loved in such a miserable state and to be so helpless to change the situation made me think, "I can't stop my wife's pain; I can't help my unborn child; I can't even prevent myself from feeling despair over how fragile and insecure my own happiness is. If only I had gotten through Mu, maybe things would be different, but now it is too late. With my wife's back so bad and a child on the way, I will never be able to attend sesshin again."

As my wife began to recover, my grief over all the wasted opportunities to get through Mu turned into a desperate wish to attend one more sesshin. "Please," I begged her, "let me go to one more sesshin. I know that you are scared about what might happen to your back while I am gone, but I'm sure you will be OK. I promise that this is the last sesshin I will ever ask to attend."

A few weeks later I was at the Rohatsu sesshin of 1974. A Rohatsu sesshin, traditionally held once a year in December, honors the deep enlightenment of Shakyamuni Buddha. The sitting schedule is even tougher than usual, and the participants resolve to exert themselves to the utmost. In preparation, I had spent every second of free time before sesshin doing zazen. I was determined to do whatever it took to get through Mu. This was my last chance, but I was more confident than desperate.

At the end of my first dokusan in sesshin, Roshi had rung his handbell and I was making my final bow before leaving the room when, to my own surprise, I heard myself exclaim, "I am going to get through Mu this sesshin. I know that I can!" "Of course you can," Roshi replied as I left. As I returned to the zendo, I thought, "No turning back now."

Maintaining one's resolve is a constant battle. Around the midpoint of the sesshin the familiar doubts began to arise when I was stretching my aching legs in the basement exercise room. "You can't really get through Mu. You have no idea what Mu is. Maybe other people do, but not you." Then I looked up at the electrical junction boxes in the unfinished ceiling of the basement, and my confidence returned. For five years I had looked at those junction boxes and thought, "Whoever did that wiring has abilities that are beyond me. I don't even know what is inside a junction box." However, in preparation for the birth of our child, I had renovated a room in the basement of our house, and in the course of installing new electric lights, I had not only found out what goes inside a junction box, I had put up a few myself. What I had thought was beyond me had turned out to be very easy. So, when the doubting voices made themselves heard, I shut them up by saying to myself, "If you can put up junction boxes, you can get through Mu."

Sesshin is a collective effort of all the participants, and this Rohatsu sesshin had extraordinary energy. The monitors were unremitting in using the kyosaku stick to encourage the sitters; I was hit so often each round that I soon stopped noticing. As my concentration and energy increased, Roshi began questioning me. I grew more and more confident that an appropriate answer would just pop out. Finally, on the last night of sesshin, Roshi said, "I am going to give you one last question; if you can answer it, you will have passed Mu. *If you returned your flesh to your mother and your bones to your father, what would Mu be?* Bring me the answer at dokusan tomorrow morning." On the last night of a sesshin, particularly Rohatsu sesshin, everyone stays up very late doing zazen. Some sit through the night. However, having stayed up late most of the previous nights of sesshin, by 10 P.M. I was falling asleep. I just couldn't concentrate on Roshi's question. Normally, I would have made myself stay up, if only out of pride at not wanting to be the first person in my room to go to bed. But this night was strangely different; instead of arguing with myself about whether or not to try to stay up late, I just went to bed. Waking unprompted after a few hours sleep, I returned to the zendo to work on the question.

At morning dokusan, I still did not have an answer. Only one more dokusan remained before the end of sesshin. I wrote a note to the monitors: "Please don't let up on me. If I don't get through Mu this sesshin, when will I?" Then, I suddenly found that I no longer cared whether or not I got though Mu. I just felt profoundly grateful to be at this sesshin, with another opportunity, in dokusan, to try to answer the question.

I skipped lunch to remain in the zendo and continue sitting. Formal zazen resumed. The blows from the kyosaku rained down on my shoulders. Roshi's handbell rung. The people in the zendo exploded out the door and up the stairs that led to the dokusan room. As I took my place in the middle of the line for dokusan, I saw the face of the person at the head of the line. It was huge and radiant. He knew what Mu was, and so did I. *But what was it?*

I kept concentrating on Mu, oblivious to the fact that I was getting closer and closer to the head of the dokusan line. Soon it would be my turn to see Roshi, but there was no space for worry to arise; there was just Mu. A bubble of laughter started forming in the pit of my stomach. I watched as it got bigger and bigger, until it finally burst forth as a huge belly laugh. Then I knew with certainty that *everything is Mu*, from getting up in the morning to going to bed at night. And when I looked for the answer to Roshi's final question, it was there too.

When I went into the dokusan room, I told Roshi what had just happened. He seemed unimpressed. I gave him my answer to his final question. He sighed. "OK," he said, "you can begin work on subsequent koans, but when you do, please try to be a little less conceptual."

I had lied to my wife. The 1974 Rohatsu sesshin was not the last that I asked her to let me attend. Early in 1975 I was back at sesshin, anxious to see what it would be like to work on koans subsequent to Mu. I was also a little apprehensive, because, although I knew that something had happened at the Rohatsu sesshin, I had no idea of exactly what it was. What did I know now that I had not known before I had been passed on Mu? The words, "Everything is Mu, from getting up in the morning to going to bed at night" were now just words. No wonder Roshi had told me to be less conceptual.

In dokusan I gave answer after answer to the first koan after Mu that I was given by Roshi, and each was rejected. I grew more and more depressed as I began to suspect that Roshi had made a big mistake in passing me on Mu. Soon he would realize his mistake and send me back to working on Mu again. I doubted that I could ever again muster the determination that had allowed me work on Mu the way I had at the previous Rohatsu sesshin.

From the depths of despair, the highest joys are born. With the resolution of my second koan, I not only experienced great joy, but I also gained a better understanding of what had happened at the Rohatsu sesshin. Concentrating so hard on Mu had led to the dropping away of my habitual thoughts, and this dropping away enabled me to experience the world of Mu directly. The world of Mu turned out to be none

Tall Branches, Tender Leaves

other than the one in which I had always lived, but seen through different eyes.

That second koan marked the beginning of my love affair with koans. I found that the subsequent koans I was given were powerful tools for deepening and clarifying my nonconceptual understanding of the world of Mu. I experienced a new sense of freedom. And I came to appreciate the genius of the great Zen masters who had formulated these koans.

However, practice continued to have its ups and downs. When things went well, I was in heaven; when they went poorly, I was in hell. If I got stuck on a koan, and my answers in dokusan were rejected, my self-confidence would evaporate. I would again fall into thinking, "There must be something that I did not learn when I was passed on Mu, and this must be what is preventing me from getting the answer to this koan." However, when I did get the answer, often by Roshi leading me to it (or shoving my face into it), I would realize yet again that there was nothing that I had needed to know which I did not already know, in order to have solved the koan on my own. After a while, I came to trust that this was so. If I put myself squarely into the koan, the way an actor throws himself totally into a role, the answer was invariably right there in front of me, even though I might not see it at first.

My love affair with koans continued over the years, but my passion for them began to flag as I became aware of some problems in my practice. For example, I knew that koans were training devices and that it was the process of solving them, rather than their solution, that was most important. However, I liked the sense of achievement that came with passing koans. Through a mixture of pride and impatience, I wanted to add more koans to the list of those that I had already passed. I was in such a hurry that now when I review certain koans I cannot remember what the answers to them were.

A second problem was that during sesshin I spent a lot of time thinking about how to present my answers to each koan, which usually require some kind of demonstration rather than a mere verbal response. This type of problem solving was seductive, very much like what I did in my chemistry research. However, I missed the one-pointed, nonconceptual concentration that I had worked so hard to develop when I was struggling with Mu. At sesshin my favorite rounds of zazen became those immediately after dokusans in which I had been passed on a koan, before I began work on the next koan, because I could just do zazen without thinking about anything.

BORDEN

An aspect of koans that I found increasingly disturbing was how little they seemed to relate to the way I led my everyday life. There may have been more connections than I realized, but, for whatever reasons, I did not put forth the effort to make those connections. I have met an uncomfortably large number of Zen students who have gone very far in their koan study, but who give little outward evidence of having integrated significant benefits from koan practice into their being.

TANGEN ROSHI My practice took another turn in the autumn of 1979, when I had an opportunity to meet Harada Tangen Roshi. Tangen Roshi had been the head monk at Hosshinji when Philip Kapleau had trained there in the 1950s, and some stories about "Tangen-san" are contained in the account of "P. K." in *The Three Pillars of Zen*. Based on these stories and others I had heard from Roshi Kapleau, I expected to find a kyosaku-wielding samurai in priest's robes when I went, with considerable trepidation, to meet Tangen Roshi at his temple near Hosshinji.

I was attending a scientific conference in Kyoto. Although my ability to speak Japanese was very limited, I boarded a train that I hoped would take me to the town where Tangen Roshi's temple was located. When I got off the train, not knowing how to ask the way to the temple, I hailed a taxi. It turned out that the temple was within easy walking distance of the station.

A sesshin was in progress, so I waited outside the zendo until Tangen Roshi emerged. He seemed delighted to see me, but he took no interest in the presents that I had brought him. Instead of accepting them, he took me to the main hall and had me place them on the altar. He then lit a stick of incense, which he handed to me, signaling that I should offer it at the altar. Next, he pulled out a cushion for me and made a cup of tea. Only then did he speak.

Tangen Roshi's English was very limited, but he employed it to great effect in combination with vivid gestures. I had no difficulty understanding him. He asked how I had gotten to the temple. When I replied, "By taxi," he looked displeased. I explained that I had not known how to get from the station to his temple, and that I would be happy to return to the station by taxi. He shook his head and said, "Very easy. Come." So he led me several hundred yards from the temple, until the station came into view, making sure that I knew where to make the necessary turns, and warning me, by miming the gestures, to look carefully both ways before crossing a busy road.

Tall Branches, Tender Leaves

It seemed to me that while I was with Tangen Roshi, my welfare was the most important thing in the world to him. For example, when he showed me where I would be sleeping, he took one look at my long legs and then added another cushion and quilt to the end of the futon that had been laid out for me, to make sure that my feet did not stick out and get cold. At that moment he seemed more like a grandmother than a samurai.

However, Tangen Roshi was not just a sweet old grandmother. After showing me where the station was, on the way back to the temple he suddenly asked me, "What time is it where you live?" At first I thought I must have misunderstood him, and then I tried to remember whether I was supposed to add or subtract seven hours from the time my watch said it was in Japan, in order to convert to Seattle time. It was only after the Roshi left me that I realized, with considerable chagrin, that he had been asking a very different question from the one that I had answered.

It seemed my fate to demonstrate to Tangen Roshi what a poor Zen student I was. That same afternoon, following the chanting service in the main hall, I wandered back to the zendo and waited for zazen to resume. Soon I began to grow uneasy, because none of the other sesshin participants arrived. Just as I realized that something must be wrong, the Roshi appeared. Without a word, he led me to where the rest of the participants were waiting for me, so that they could begin eating the evening meal laid out before them.

Ordinarily, at that moment I would have wished for the Earth to open and swallow me up. However, Tangen Roshi appeared so nonjudgmental that I just accepted the fact that I had made a mistake and did not dwell on it. On the many other occasions when I answered his unexpected questions poorly or showed him how inattentive I was, I also felt that the Roshi really was like a grandmother, watching with interest what her grandchild could and could not do, but not making judgments. The Roshi's unconditional positive regard somehow made it possible for me to make mistakes and then just move on, without getting caught up in regrets or self-criticism.

An even more valuable lesson came in another visit to Tangen Roshi's temple during a very stressful period of my life. My marriage was falling apart, and my (now ex-) wife had a male friend who seemed to be replacing me in her affections. To say that I was jealous does not begin to capture the intensity of the emotions that kept flooding in on me. A few days after my arrival at the temple, the Roshi gave an encouragement talk in the zendo. As always, his resonant voice seemed to emanate from the depths of his being. Most of his talks were in Japanese, but he occasionally injected a few words of English. In the middle of this talk he broke into English and said, "Wide Mind. Wide Mind. Only wide Mind!" At these words I realized that in my own wide Mind there was not a single jealous thought, and that my feelings of jealousy came from my narrow, self-centered perspective. My wife was obviously seeking what she felt she needed, and if what she needed was no longer me, that was fundamentally OK. There have been many subsequent occasions when I have gratefully recalled not only Tangen Roshi's words but also the sound of his voice saying, "Wide Mind. Wide Mind. Only wide Mind!"

HARADA SHODO ROSHI On a cold day in the late autumn of 1988, I first met Harada Shodo Roshi, the man who became my teacher after the retirement of Roshi Kapleau. I was spending a weekend at Sogenji, Harada Roshi's temple in Okayama, Japan. The Roshi was very busy all weekend, so it was not until late Sunday afternoon that he had time to see me. As dusk fell, the Roshi, his interpreter, and I sat looking out at the temple's beautiful pond and the garden beyond, while the Roshi whisked bowls of frothy green tea for us. For a long time there was little conversation as we all watched the garden begin to fade into darkness. When the Roshi broke the silence, he asked me to take some red leaves from the Japanese maple by the side of the pond to a student of his in Seattle. I had expected the Roshi to tell the translator to get the leaves, so I was surprised when he himself went out into the cold night to fetch them.

When the Roshi returned, I told him that I had heard that he was planning to establish a Zen training center in Seattle and eventually move there. I asked him why he wanted to relocate to a foreign country when Sogenji was such a magnificent place to train students. He replied matter-of-factly, "Because it is important, before leaving this world, to create something that was not here when I arrived." Something about the simplicity and sincerity of his reply caused me to blurt out, "What can I do to help you?" In reply, he did not say, "Donate money" or "Help build a Zen group in Seattle." He just said, "Do zazen."

So I did zazen in Seattle with a student of Harada Shodo Roshi, and the next fall the Roshi came to conduct a sesshin. The first sesshin he gave in America was held in a small house that his student had rented.

Tall Branches, Tender Leaves

conducted in a tin tool shed in the backyard. The roof was so low that
I banged my head on it every time I stood up, causing the whole shed
to shake. Yet the Roshi's presence transformed the tool shed into a
sanzen room.

In the dim light of a single candle he was half in shadow, doing zazen
with a tautness and energy born of decades of monastic training. When
I entered the room, the Roshi reminded me of a large cat—completely
still and apparently oblivious to my presence, but actually aware of my
every motion. And I sensed that, like being too close to a tiger, what
might happen was unpredictable and potentially very dangerous.

Harada Roshi's responses in sanzen to my demonstrations of koans
have run the gamut from a scathing, "Really, Wes, that was pitiful" to
"Not bad," accompanied by a smile so big that it lights up the sanzen
room. The first few times I saw that radiant smile, I thought, "I have
passed this koan." However, this apparent sign of approval is almost
always followed by a pithy clarification or a clue indicating a different
direction in which to look. Often the Roshi says, "To demonstrate this
koan, you must go to that place where there is no shadow of self." The
Roshi seems to attach at least as much importance to the mind-state I
bring to sanzen as to the answers I present.

"Be careful what you wish for, because you may get it" is an adage
that applies to my koan practice with Harada Roshi. Ten years ago I
wished that passing koans would somehow become less important to me
than using each koan to deepen my zazen. Without my asking, Harada
Roshi has given me my wish. He made me work a long time on the first
koan that he gave me, so long that I stopped consciously searching for
an answer. Both in and out of sesshin, I just counted my breath. Then
one morning in sanzen the Roshi unexpectedly gave me the answer. To
my surprise, it was not very different from the first answer I had given
him more than two years before.

Throughout my life, it seems that I have been given the type of teaching
and training that I needed. Although I fervently wish that my family had
been spared the immense suffering that my father's manic-depressive illness produced, I believe that there is a causal relationship between this
suffering and my desire for spiritual training. When I was a teenager, had

I not been told to read *Siddhartha* by a girl with whom I was infatuated, I doubt I would have picked up the book. Though I went to England to learn theoretical chemistry, I encountered Vipassana meditation there. Subsequently, Mrs. March showed me that spiritual work involves much more than sitting quietly in meditation. Without these experiences, I would not have been attracted by *The Three Pillars of Zen*, nor able to endure the rigors of the Zen training offered by Roshi Kapleau at the Rochester Zen Center.

I am profoundly grateful to Roshi Kapleau, not only for writing the book and being my first Zen teacher, but also for showing me how to practice with an intensity that I never knew I could muster. When he called me a "spiritual butterfly" during my first sesshin, his arrow went deep. In motivating his students to put all of themselves into their practice, with nothing held back, Roshi Kapleau was adept in what Buddhism calls "skillful means."

The koan training that I received from Roshi Kapleau, after I got through Mu, was rewarding in many ways, and it motivated me to continue to attend sesshin. Yasutani Roshi, the teacher under whom Roshi Kapleau did the bulk of his own koan training, reportedly said that koans are sometimes like the candy one feeds to children to keep them happy—without koans, many Zen students would not have the determination to keep practicing seriously. Koans worked that way for me. With my high "need for achievement," the sweet taste of passing koans kept me coming back for more.

When I began my Zen training I hoped that by practicing zazen I was going to get something called "enlightenment." It took many years for me to begin to realize that the purpose of Zen training is not to acquire enlightenment but to shave away ego-centered thoughts until one is able to see that fundamentally one lacks nothing. Since then my Zen practice has largely consisted of repeated, breath-to-breath attempts to clear away the mental clutter that obscures the marvelously wide, mirror-like Mind with which we are all endowed. During the past thirty years the giraffe has nibbled contentedly on the tender leaves of one tall tree, and the butterfly has sipped sweet nectar from a single flower.

Tall Branches, Tender Leaves

3 | What's the Difference Between a Buddhist and a Non-Buddhist?

CASEY FRANK

W hen Sister Regina Paul stood before our fourth grade class at Saint Margaret's parochial school, with her black and white habit and categorical teaching, she was the embodiment of sartorial and pedagogical *chiaroscuro*. Sister Regina Paul was my first cousin, but it never helped—in fact, she always gave me extra homework because I was a member of *la familia*. One day in that class, a gleaming image of the Buddha appeared in our textbook. Like a letter from home, it made an indelible impression on my young heart. Sister Regina Paul couldn't have known what an impact it would have.

Catholicism was my first religious love. Like other first loves, it is part of me. From a time before my earliest memories, I went to church virtually every day, and loved it. What's not to love when you know the way to heaven? But at age fifteen it suddenly hit me that the teachers were not talking from experience. They did not personally know the truth of which they spoke. I felt betrayed.

Fortunately, bodhisattvas emerge when needed. While I was attending a Jesuit high school, my friend David's mother gave him a copy of *The Three Pillars of Zen*. We read it from cover to cover and rapped about it. The first edition, written in Japan, did not mention a Rochester Zen Center. I was in Buffalo and assumed that Philip Kapleau was still in Japan. I read everything in print on Zen, and spent a couple of years sampling Scientology, Transcendental Meditation, and Hare Krishna, the few nontraditional options one had in Buffalo in the late sixties.

Eventually I bought a new edition of *The Three Pillars*. On the back cover I discovered that Philip Kapleau was merely a bus ride away. As they say, when the student is ready, the teacher appears. I signed up for a Zen workshop on July 3, 1969. In the afternoon session, Roshi Kapleau had me sit up front (my boredom must have showed). Yet even through my haze, I felt a surge of spiritual optimism. During the one-on-one interviews Roshi conducted afterwards, he asked me, "Have you ever done any building?" "Sure, I can do that," I responded enthusiastically. (Not true.) But I showed up in Rochester anyway, joined the staff program, and began to learn carpentry. I soon discovered that I detested seated meditation. I thought it was cruel, and believed that nobody could be less suited to it than me. But after thirty days at the Zen Center, I told myself, "You'll never forgive yourself if you leave this place now. You've got to plumb this to its depths."

When I first went to the Rochester Zen Center, my parents were distraught. They had novenas said for the salvation of my soul, and had the parish priest call to try and talk me out of it. If I had been in jail it would not have been as bad. I had been taught that I could do *anything* and be forgiven, anything except leave the church. That's the one thing that is fatal. Next stop, hell.

Taking a chance, I asked my parents to allow Roshi to visit their home when he was in Buffalo to conduct a workshop. Their response was, "All right, we'll do it, but don't expect to covert us." My intuitive mother told me later that as soon as she saw Roshi, she knew he was a good person, and her doubts fell away. They have been fond of each other ever since. My siblings were also there to check out the Zen master. Roshi was talking with Mom and my brothers and sisters, smoothing the waters, but my father was still holding back. The conversation somehow veered to the war in Vietnam. Dad said: "Well, at least our motives are good." Roshi responded, "Our motives are good, ha! All we want is to swell our own national ego, and we're willing to murder men, women, and children nine thousand miles away to do it."

I was frozen. I knew that my father was about to stand up and say, "Get out!" But instead my father answered, "Yeah...you're right, I don't

What's the Difference Between a Buddhist and a Non-Buddhist?

know why I said such a thing.... Well, how did you get interested in Zen anyway?" *What?* My parents decided to accompany us to the workshop. My father sat in a nice half-lotus as if he had been doing it for years. From then on things became much more harmonious.

Being at the Zen Center sparked an unanticipated reconciliation with my born faith. I noted the enlightenment story in *The Three Pillars* in which the writer had gone through a "total rejection of Christianity" at the same age I had. I thus felt I had company, and began to see common ground. Elsewhere in the book, Yasutani Roshi cites contemplative Christianity as an example of *gedo* (non-Buddhist) Zen. Though I was clueless about both, this comparison lessened the gap I perceived between between East and West. Moreover, when Roshi Kapleau spoke of Christianity, he did so with genuine, nonsectarian respect.

The Three Pillars of Zen stresses the importance of faith to a degree that seems compatible with Catholic teaching, at least in principle. Faith (*daishinkon*) is the first of the three essentials of Zen practice. Yasutani Roshi is unequivocal when he states that without faith, "it is impossible to progress far in one's practice," or as my Italian grandparents might have said, *è impossibile progredire nella pratica*. In Zen, the first meaning of faith is faith in our own buddha nature, as exemplified by Shakyamuni's enlightenment.

"ARE YOU STILL A CATHOLIC?" I ended up spending nineteen years in Rochester, almost half the time as a member of the Center's resident staff. Throughout the years my personal "Buddhist-Christian dialogue" continued.

Once, when Roshi was conducting a Zen workshop at Canisius College in Buffalo, a diminutive young woman came up to me and said, "Casey dear, how are you?" She gave me a big hug and asked, "Don't you recognize me?" I replied, "Nooo..." She continued, "I'm Joan Wagner. I used to be Sister Mary Mathias, your third grade teacher. I'm still a nun, but we don't wear the habit anymore. I wanted to come to the Zen workshop, and I heard from your mom that you were going to be here." Soon about sixty people were doing *zazen* (meditation), and I was patrolling with the *kyosaku* (encouragement stick). Joan Wagner was sitting in a beautiful full-lotus posture. She raised her hands, asking to be struck. I went to hit her gently and dispassionately, but suddenly all the years of corporal punishment by the nuns and priests flashed into my body-mind, staggering me. In your wildest fantasy as a kid, could you imagine that the stern teacher was going to sit down and ask you to hit her with a stick? Impossible. But there she was. I stepped back, took a deep breath, and gave her a vigorous smack.

At one point in the early years of the Zen Center, Roshi decided to move to Naples, New York, and train only monks. There were already two, named Sojun and Sozan, along with three other people who had announced that they wanted to be ordained. Since that was where the action was, I wanted to become a monk too. Roshi made me meditate on it, and get my parents' approval. They thought about it and concluded, "Well, our first choice would be to have a Jesuit in the family, but, failing that, a Zen monk is pretty good." Handling the decision in this way had a salutary effect on my family, who felt included in the process. My grandmother came up to me after my ordination ceremony and said: "It's not like the Latin Mass, it's weird to me. But that Roshi, he's a holy man." Years later, she asked me, "When I die, I know I'm going to see Jesus. Am I also going to see Buddha?" I told her, "If you really want to see Buddha, you'll see Buddha too." Then she asked, "Are you still a Catholic?" I replied, "I'm not 'not a Catholic' like I need to reject Catholicism, but it would be unfair to practicing Catholics were I to say, 'I'm a Catholic.'"

During the time that I was a monk, I was in Buffalo on Zen Center business when I espied my chemistry teacher from high school, a Jesuit priest, waiting at a bus stop. I pulled over, and we spoke for a half-hour about my Zen practice and his teaching career. As I was about to leave, he said, "Before you go, let me ask you one question. At least you haven't lost your Catholic faith, have you?" I replied, "Father, how could you ask such a question?" When I told Roshi of this exchange, he laughed and said, "That rock-bottom faith that you could remain a Catholic even if you're a Zen monk, in fact no matter what else you are, is very profound too."

I trained as a monk named Sokei Shakya for two years. It was hard getting used to not going home to visit family, harder even than being celibate. During that period, difficult as it was, I also experienced the great joy of being a "homeless one," knowing in a new way that there is nothing to lose. I did not have a family to lose, nor possessions, nor hair. This engendered a freedom that I had never experienced.

Being a monk is a mode of practice in which you work from the form to the substance. The form helps you come to realization. At its best, monasticism is neither a lifestyle nor an end in itself. As the Chinese master T'ui-yin said, "Becoming a monk. . . is for the sake of becoming

What's the Difference Between a Buddhist and a Non-Buddhist?

free from the tyranny of birth and death; it is to continue the *prajna*
[wisdom] life of the Buddha; it is to deliver all beings from their trans-
migration in the triple world."[1] I saw harmony between these aspirations
and the life of monks such as Saint Anthony of the Desert, from Egypt.
Anthony struggled powerfully with obstructions to his quest in a manner
reminiscent of the Buddha's confrontation with the demon Mara.
When Anthony testified in the cathedral in Alexandria and changed the
course of Western history, he vividly demonstrated his realization and
the fruit of his monasticism.[2]

Roshi's plans to build a monastery did not pan out, and the would-be
monks changed their minds. After the other monks resigned, I told
Roshi, "I'm quitting." He said flatly, "No, you can't." I asked incredu-
lously, "What do you mean, no? The other monks quit. Why can't I?" He
said, "You can't quit because you don't know *why* you want to. You're just
having an emotional outburst." He assigned me the question, "Why am
I a monk?" as a koan. I worked on it for months, and began to understand
why I was *not* a monk. I had become a monk to practice in harmony with
a monastic community where we could support one another, while
learning to deal with the inevitable few who won't wash their own dirty
dishes. Monasticism needs a community of monks, which in turn needs
the support of the laity. When both factors are missing, lay practice is
best. That's our world, and it again became mine.

A few years later, my fourteen-year-old brother Anthony became ill
with meningitis. Before we knew it, he was in a coma, dying. I recall
standing with my cousin Sister Regina Paul at Anthony's bedside, chanting and praying together, the three of us in communion. This experience epitomized for me the intersection of all people and paths. People
are born, die, long for transcendence, and need compassion. Yet, on
another level, a glaring divide was evident. During the traumatic weeks
between the onset of Anthony's illness and his death, the "great matter"
(as it is called in Buddhism) was right in front of the family. When the
raw truth confronted us, Catholicism provided a palliative to the pain —
but also an anesthesia that masked an opportunity for insight. "It's God's
will." "God wanted Tony in heaven with him." This orientation is under-
standable, but it short-circuits spiritual questioning. In contrast, Zen
training provides the strength and clarity to embrace death directly, and
thus see through it. As Abraham a Sancta Clara has stated, "He who dies
before he dies, does not die when he dies."[3] That is not to say I wasn't
deeply saddened by Tony's death.

FRANK

A related issue came to a boil when my mother was in serious pain following back surgery. I brought her *The Way of the Pilgrim* (which Roshi had given me), and suggested that the book's Jesus prayer might help her focus her mind and transcend her pain, at least to some degree. She started practicing this venerable mantra and found great relief. Yet my father said, "That kind of thing may be fine for Buddhists, but we Christians were made to suffer. And Jesus is the supreme example. He died on the cross suffering."

Although Buddhism also teaches that suffering characterizes the human condition, it equally stresses the cessation of suffering. Once, when visiting the beautiful cathedral in Santa Fe, New Mexico, I sought out the monsignor in charge and told him that one of the stations of the cross was missing. These stations, found in most Catholic churches, depict the trial, suffering, and crucifixion of Jesus. They are portrayed in a dramatic and sanguinary fashion. The monsignor glanced around, eyed me skeptically, and asked, "Which one?" I replied, "The resurrection. What is the point of all this suffering unless it leads to transcendence?"

In the 1980s, I worked for several years in grassroots peace politics. Often the escalating arms race would bring Rochester's religions together in an exceptional unity of purpose, such as when virtually all of them endorsed the nuclear freeze campaign in 1984. I spoke at meetings of just about every denomination, often to initiate the formation of a peace group within a congregation. For a time, I made no reference to my religious affiliation, not wanting to be a missionary. But this proved unsatisfactory, so I learned to refer matter-of-factly to my Zen background, and move on. People use that type of knowledge to relate to others, perhaps at the risk of prejudice, but also in good faith. Still, at ecumenical gatherings, I often ended up in back grousing with the University of Rochester Jewish chaplain, Rabbi Paul Glaser, about "Jesus this, Jesus that." For most of our Christian brethren, religion = Christianity = Jesus.

SPRING WATER AND SACRAMENTAL WINE   The late Jesuit priest Enomiya Lassalle was a longtime Zen practitioner, a friend of Roshi Kapleau, and a pioneer in the dialogue between Zen and Catholicism. Once, when he visited the Rochester Zen Center, he stated, "Zen is like fresh mountain spring water; anyone can drink of it and be refreshed." I respectfully replied, "Yes, Father, but if you mix anything with spring water—even sacramental wine—then it's not spring

What's the Difference Between a Buddhist and a Non-Buddhist?

water anymore." Therein lies the problem. The admixture of Zen and Catholicism as promoted by Catholic clergy begets a hybrid inappropriate to both traditions. That is why Roshi, while never criticizing the personal *practice* of Zen by other clergy, has been strongly critical of Catholic priests and nuns who are sanctioned as Zen teachers.

Catholic clergy must take vows to uphold Catholic dogma. They are formal representatives of a teaching that is fundamentally different from Zen. For example, in Catholicism the Church is supposed to determine the content of belief:

> There is nothing ambiguous about how a Catholic knows what to believe: whatever the Church proposes as having been revealed.... Then, to remove every shade of ambiguity, Catholics are informed how the Church offers her adherents the word of God.[4]

This is a vertical, authority-based, ecclesiastical structure. In stark contrast, the Buddha's reported last words were: "Be ye lamps unto yourself. Be ye refuges unto yourself.... Look not for refuge to anyone besides yourself."[5] Institutional Buddhism (including Zen) certainly has its share of dogma and hierarchy. But profound questioning, the "great doubt," is a crucial, even a defining feature of the Zen taught by Roshi Kapleau, in the spirit of Zen ancestors such as Bassui and Hakuin.

Another fundamental difference is found in interpretations of human responsibility. The Church holds that God is the creator of the universe, including us, and that his will governs all events. As Saint Augustine asserted, "With regard to the divine will, remember that it is not like ours.... To effects which he wills to be necessary, God provides necessary causes."[6] This can be contrasted with the Buddhist teaching of karma, which holds that we are the principal architects of our own fate. The Christian view of God's role corresponds to what the Japanese call *tariki*, or other-power. When salvation depends largely on one's own efforts, that is *jiriki*, or self-power. Ultimately, Zen is beyond both. Roshi once put it well when he declared, "Having gained some understanding, I knew that God is neither good nor almighty nor anything else. In fact, God is not even God."[7]

It is not enough for Catholic clergy, personally in their hearts, to reinterpret "God" as "buddha nature" and "Christ" as "bodhisattva." Catholic clergy have inherited a long and great tradition that has its own rationale and methodology. Zen presented under the penumbra of the Catholic Church has inappropriate associations that do not benefit seek-

FRANK

ers of the Buddha Way, nor do justice to Catholicism. Did Saint Francis of Assisi need Zen? Did Saint Teresa of Avila? Of course not. They traveled within their tradition. If Catholic clergy do not represent this view, why remain as its formal standard bearers? If they do believe in it, they should not also assert they are representatives of Zen. Zen is like fresh mountain spring water, and those who thirst will be able to drink more deeply if each religious tradition carries forth its own noble and unique values.

On one occasion, when Roshi and I were in New Mexico, we visited an extraordinary Catholic priory called Christ in the Desert (a priory is a small monastery). It was a joint Trappist-Benedictine venture in a fabulous setting, the juncture of two mesas along the Chama River. Some of the monks practiced zazen; they had a *zendo* (meditation hall) set up where they said their morning office. Roshi and the prior had a heart-to-heart discussion; Roshi gave a talk to the monks and other visitors; and for a few days we all went to Mass, meals, and work together. I still correspond by e-mail with Brother Christopher, the guest master. During the visit, Roshi and I noticed that the priory had a Buddhist chanting instrument, a large bowl-shaped metal bell called a *keisu*. It sat on the floor in the foyer, filled with umbrellas. At Roshi's urging, I approached Christopher: "Brother, that's a sacred liturgical instrument, and it shouldn't be used like that." He replied delightedly, "Aw Case, you can have it!" However, we found out why he was only the guest master when the prior corrected the offer, saying the bell had been a gift and they couldn't part with it. Later, the instrument was moved to the chapel and placed next to the altar.

The last morning at the priory, we attended the daily pre-dawn service. Though I had been to thousands of Masses, this one proved cathartic. When the priest held up the consecrated wafer and wine, exhorting us to eat the body of Christ and drink the blood of Christ, I got physically ill. The bloody imagery made me nauseous, and I wanted to leave. Roshi grabbed me by the arm, restraining me. I croaked, "That's disgusting— eat and drink from his body?! Roshi, what does it mean?" He whispered, "Hang in there, and when we're outside I will explain it to you."

When we emerged, I demanded his response. He said, "It's pure cannibalism." I cracked up laughing. Later we discussed more nuanced interpretations of the doctrine of transubstantiation, and I appreciate the significance it holds for Catholics. Yet I am still struck

What's the Difference Between a Buddhist and a Non-Buddhist?

by the primal coarseness of the ritual. Can you imagine drinking the blood of the Buddha as a spiritual practice? Or of George Washington as a patriotic one?

By this point I had learned something of Roshi's own religious background, and I recognized some continuities. As a schoolboy, Philip Kapleau had stubbornly refused to attend church because of the contradictions that troubled his questioning mind. Catholic, Protestant, and Jewish clergy whom he consulted left him unsatisfied. In high school he formed an Atheists Club. The year was 1928, three years after the infamous Scopes trial, and the principal used the threat of expulsion to make Kapleau disband the club.

I recall another edifying visit to a Catholic community: Madonna House in Ontario, Canada. This time my companion was a fellow Zen student. We walked in unannounced. The director, an extraordinary woman who was a former Russian baroness, exclaimed, "Well, you finally arrived! For years I've been praying for the Lord to send a Zen monk to visit. Zen needs to know more about Christianity—after all, this is a Christian culture—and Lord knows Christianity can learn a lot from Zen." After a couple of days at Madonna House, we felt wonderfully gratified, not because the Christians and the Buddhists had all blended into one religion, but because we mutually appreciated our different approaches to spirituality.

The movement for cultural diversity is a good model to emulate in these interactions. We must overcome our antipathy to other cultures— and other religions—not only by recognizing commonality, but also by respecting uniqueness. This is a middle way which avoids religious sectarianism and celebrates each religion's special contributions to the welfare of humanity. The Dalai Lama, when asked about the assimilation of different religions, did not assert the superiority of his own path or embrace attempts to merge disparate traditions. He said:

> Forming a new world religion is difficult and not particularly desirable. However, in that love is essential to all religions, one could speak of the universal religion of love. As for the techniques and methods for developing love as well as for achieving salvation or permanent liberation, there are many differences between religions. Thus, I do not think we could make one philosophy or one religion. Furthermore, I think that differences in faith are useful. There is a

FRANK

richness in the fact that there are so many different presentations of the way. Given that there are so many different types of people with various predispositions and inclinations, this is helpful.[8]

It is certainly the case that Zen masters, Christian mystics, Sufi adepts within Islam, and mystical Hassidim within Judaism all have a bond to one another. In some ways, that bond may be as meaningful as the links to their respective parent religions. Human nature is what it is, and its uncovering must share common characteristics on the level of deep experience. Yet, our ability to travel into the depths of our nature is related to the orientation of the religious path we choose. How we subsequently express any insights likewise depends on our religious culture. When it has been suggested to Roshi that "all religions are one," his response has been, "One what?"

For many Buddhists today, the most troublesome quality of Catholicism (and certain other Christian sects) is the missionary mentality. From the time Europeans first sailed the oceans, Catholic missionaries worked hand in glove with colonial powers in the destruction of indigenous non-Christian cultures around the world. This is not just ancient history. Well into the twentieth century, church-run schools attempted to make native American, Canadian, and Australian children into good Christians, forbidding the practice of indigenous religions and the speaking of native languages. In Vietnam in 1963, two Catholic leaders, Archbishop Thuc and his brother President Diêm, outlawed the celebration of the most important Buddhist holiday in Vietnam, Wesak. In 1987, a Vatican spokesman said that Judaism finds its "ultimate fulfillment in Christianity." One of Pope John Paul II's recent best sellers, *Crossing the Threshold of Hope*, unambiguously denigrates Buddhism as inferior.

Still, in the final analysis, it is best to seek reconciliation. A mutually respectful approach is also in keeping with the teachings of *The Three Pillars of Zen* and Roshi Kapleau. In my family's case, the pièce de résistance in Zen-Catholic diplomacy came when Roshi returned from Mexico and presented my parents with two beautiful crucifixes he had bought, one rosewood and one silver. They were deeply touched by this gesture of affection and respect.

Perhaps the most promising commonalities between Catholicism and Zen can be found on a political and social level. I admire the current Pope as a great peacemaker. His consistent opposition to military aggression, principled rejection of the death penalty, and strong advocacy of

social justice are worthy of emulation. Buddhists can stand shoulder to
shoulder with him on these issues.

My mother is a big fan of Mother Cabrini, a noted Catholic educator who has a popular memorial near my present home in Denver. The water from the spring on the site of the memorial is prized as having curative powers, and Mom likes to give this water to her sick friends, sometimes in the hospital. I bring her refills when I visit. She guilelessly asked me, "Do you believe that this water can help cure people?" I said, "With the love that you transmit through this water, it's the milk of human kindness. It can only help." We can all be friends about this. As Einstein advised, "Remember your humanity, and forget the rest."

The Three Pillars of Zen is a genetic map of buddha nature, a birth certificate for a life lived to high purpose, a preamble to teaching by living. In *The Three Pillars*, Philip Kapleau talked the talk, and in the years that followed he walked the walk. I suspect that if Roshi and Saint Francis of Assisi were ever to get together, they would end up strolling down the street arm in arm, sharing a hearty laugh.

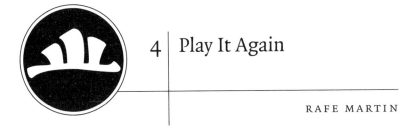

4 | Play It Again

RAFE MARTIN

In 1967, I was a graduate student of English literature at the University of Toronto. I had been drawn there, across the border, because of my interest in taking courses with the great literary critic Northrop Frye. Toronto, still a fine city now, was terrific then. It had many parks, big beautifully tended ones and countless smaller neighborhood oases and playgrounds. The city offered a good transit system, excellent bookstores and shopping, a bustling pedestrian life, richly ethnic communities, wonderful restaurants, and streets safe to walk even at night. The Vietnam War draft had swelled the population of expatriate Americans. Every evening the cafés were in full swing, psychedelia in and on the air.

One day a friend said, "You should read *The Three Pillars of Zen*. I just feel it's the book for you." My wife Rose and I had never heard this particular title, but we knew something of Zen. I had read Alan Watts's books in college, had even had lunch with him when he came to speak at our school. I was studying myth and literature, and Zen seemed to be so close to all I was reading. And, of course, it was the sixties. The flowers, trees, and skies declared, "Wake up. We're all still here."

Rose and I bought the book and read it. It poured into us like honey, every word. It was so clear and sure, so well written. We both began immediately to meditate—do *zazen*—in our tiny attic apartment. We already had a plywood door on the floor, with a fabric-covered foam pad on top, that served as our couch. We sat on this self-made couch, facing a wall. An image of a smiling, meditating Shiva hung above us. A small black metal Buddha sat on the carved Indian rosewood table nearby. Sweet incense smoke rose. We continued smoking our good herbs daily, but we also sat for five or ten minutes a day. I don't remember if we ever did more than that. But we did it each day. Interestingly, not one of our friends of the time responded to *The Three Pillars* at all.

I began following the breath while not sitting—while walking, eating, reading, writing. Nothing seemed to impede the practice. The world was vast and wide. Yet I wish there had been a little more information in *The Three Pillars* about when and when not to follow the breath. It was not entirely clear how to make use of the elements of practice in a life. What did Philip Kapleau, writing from Japan, know about the actual daily habits of a twenty-something in the sixties? I told myself, "Why stop? There is no self. Nothing can get lost." When momentary doubts arose, I would push on, either with the breath or by questioning "Who?"

Convinced that I was on the Buddha Way, I ignored signs that I was out of my depth and might need guidance. Months went by. And, given a talent for excess, I managed to get lost, totally, painfully lost. So much water flowed under that bridge. Hey! There goes the car, the career, the brain.... I left graduate school, Toronto, and friends. I left the next thing and the next. Then, through a series of karmic coincidences, the author of that life-changing, life-threatening book became my teacher. Rose and I moved to Rochester to be near the Zen Center that Philip Kapleau had founded in 1966. Our first child, Jake, was barely eight weeks old.

We put a roof over our heads by opening a bookstore. I became a storyteller. In part, this new vocation arose from having children. They made me take stock, engage life fully again, and open up the old store-house of ancient wishes, aspirations, vows, and dreams. In part, too, it came from finding myself through *The Three Pillars* and its teachings. Sensei Philip Kapleau (later to be Roshi) and the practice of zazen had revealed a traditional and timeless world, a world in which a storyteller could actually be a life role. The Zen Center and the community that formed around it became my spiritual home.

MARTIN

We usually do not associate zazen with storytelling, but in my case the two were linked. (Now I also see that *The Three Pillars* is full of stories.) Through the daily practice of attention, of zazen, the inessential was simplified out of my life. What remained was a fascination with language and a deep interest in the power of story and voice. My children helped me enter literature and the world of traditional tales via the red chambers of the heart rather than along the more palely coiled paths of the brain. Thanks to zazen, I had the attention to give the words space to arise and move and breathe.

The Zen Center was also my place of initiation. Robert Bly and the men's movement speak of a need today for genuine life-and-death initiation, and for intimate guidance from seasoned elders. In a Zen *sesshin* (meditation retreat), working one on one with a teacher, these things really exist. Initiation traditionally involves some degree of danger. Fundamental elements of life and death are purposefully focused to bring about a change of understanding and perception, a change of one's sense of self. There are ceremonial aspects too, imparting a startlingly familiar sense of the ancient and numinous. One remembers, as it were, rather than simply discovers. In the old Zen Buddhist way of sesshin, all such elements come together harmoniously. During the seventies, when war and disco was all our culture seemed to offer, the intense spiritual struggle of Zen training was like being in some ancient pit, some underground kiva, a place of initiation marked by blood, sweat, and tears. It felt very real and very good. I think of Wallace Stevens's line from *Credences of Summer:* "The utmost must be and is, good." It was like that.

In those early days, facing the roshi in *dokusan* (the private master-student encounter) was a real test of courage too. What could be more terrifying than confronting—squarely, unflinchingly—oneself? Roshi's words in dokusan could almost always be boiled down to either "Work harder" or "Good!" Pushing off from just those two points of reference, one could enter new, wider worlds. Work harder! Good! Under all the struggles of Zen practice, to be recognized again and again in so many guises, is the fear of death. And beneath that lies the deeply ingrained sense of "me," of "my," the one afraid to die. But what is *that?* Work harder! Good!

Those early sesshins were at the same time a bizarre pastiche of terror, chaos, and cosmic hysteria. Hardly "retreats," they emphasized a practice style of struggle and attack, a valiant, sword-drawn, bugle-blowing charge over the hill. But sesshin also helped engender the release of fundamental stores of strength and fearlessness, compassion and wisdom. One always emerged reconfirmed as a human being able to endure, if not triumph. Practice tapped an unusual power, the power that comes from facing fears and limits and transcending them. The Buddha's mythic tale of home-leaving, when he followed an inner call along "a road he knew not of," became one's own life story.

But it was rough on kids. Children, the few that there were at that time, saw their parents taking risks for something that entailed deep, passionate belief. The organizational structures imported from Japan, the outer containers of transformation, were stiff, hierarchical, and non-familial. We were a community, or almost a community, of those who had fought in the trenches of sesshin together. But what about family and those tender, wonderful baby-beings? Where did Winnie the Pooh fit into the samurai-like world of Zen? The priority was the attainment of *kensho* (initial enlightenment) as the foundation of a life on the Way. At the time, an "ordinary" life seemed a little too tame. I can't but feel a kind of shrinking within when I recall the times when a child's voice was not allowed to disrupt a ceremony or muddy the (assumed) purity of practice. Desperation, I now see, played itself out in many forms. The meditators who sat perfectly upright were as mad in their own ways as the parents tormented by their inability to do more zazen or hear more Dharma talks. "Yikes!" as my now-grown son used to say. Yikes.

Trying hard, working hard on our all-important practice, we often goofed as parents. Not only were the responsibilities of parenting almost overwhelming, but we were also attempting to sit as much as monks do. We were trying to do two complete things at the same time. Yet what would our lives have been *without* the practice? Painful, any way you cut it. We were quite young, the war was still on, and America was a terribly confusing place. We wanted something more. We thought that if only we could work hard enough, then maybe, *maybe* the Golden Age of Zen, the glory days of T'ang-era China, might return. Well, my kids, at any rate, seem to have forgiven us amiably enough. They get that we were simply doing the best that we could.

The young people drawn to the Zen Center then were desperately trying to fit inside *The Three Pillars of Zen*, trying to remake reality to match those clear, inspiring, Japanese-flavored pages. We wanted something neater and safer than this messy world. The vision offered by *The Three Pillars*—that enlightenment and spiritual development were truly possible for us—seemed more clear-cut and less risky than the chaotic daily realities of the seventies. But you cannot recreate someone else's experience of Japanese Zen. And you cannot duplicate someone else's enlightenment, no matter how many times you read about such experiences in a book. The words fall apart in the end. Even when a trustworthy narrative emerges from life, it is so much less than the thing itself. Our attempts to fit inside a book were bound to fail.

These days, I believe it wiser to take a regular dose (but not an overdose) of zazen, and leave a lot of the rest alone. Is it simply a form of self-deception, of "ego," to say, "I'll take some of this, and not that"? I don't think so. The process of Americanizing and personalizing Zen is the bodhisattva Manjushri coming down off his lion and saying, "Hello." The work of making Zen our own is the bodhisattva Avalokiteshvara extending one of her many, many hands.

Since those early days, my understanding of *The Three Pillars* has changed and evolved. Zen does not seem so special anymore. When I reread *The Three Pillars* now, it seems so concentrated and so Japanese, so very full of the culture and atmosphere and style of a specific long-rooted tradition. But as I read I am always struck again by its unique authority and power, by its promise of transformation, and by its commitment to transmission. There are lines that perfectly evoke the experience of Zen and proclaim a realm where we all yet hope to hang our hats.

For me now, the essence of it seems simpler than it did in those early days. It is about living with some degree of grace, humor, and freedom from endless selfishness. It is about living with greater creativity, confidence, and love. And perhaps dying in this way too. This "Zen" transcends itself. *The Three Pillars* returns us from deadness to life—to the breeze and the fluttering leaves, to the flap of crows and laughter at twilight, to the daily miracles and tiny, ordinary blessings.

Recently, during a period of walking meditation at an all-day sitting, my eye strayed to the altar. An encouragement stick lay against the polished wood. Incense smoke rose. I was struck again by the elegance of the tradition. While that may sound like an aesthetic statement, it's not how I mean it. I was struck with gratitude for the way things are.

So, gratitude to *The Three Pillars*, to the teachings, and to all the people who have embodied those teachings. They have given us a great gift. There are few truly life-changing books, books for which one is eternally grateful. To call a book life-changing may sound like hyperbole, but *The Three Pillars of Zen* really was—and is—such a book. My hope is that it will someday come out in a new, illustrated edition, with commentary that accounts for the last thirty-plus years of Western and American practice. Such an edition could make a place for family and children; for cookouts and camp outs and earning-a-living Zen; for time in therapy and the unhappiness of failed marriages; for career disappointments, failed businesses, aging, and the general environmental and political bad news of our "interesting" times.

And then let's move on. Warrior Zen is necessary at times. But how about Birdsong Zen? Lover Zen? Good-food Zen? For starters. There might even be enough challenge and rigor in these paths to please the sternest soul. Effort is of many kinds; ferocity need not be the benchmark. (Relative) absence of self will do quite well.

Despite the pain of many awful mistakes, and the ease with which *The Three Pillars* compounded some of my own tendencies to err, I would do it over again if I had to. When I have to, I should say. One hundred years from now, I expect that a descendant of the book will be waiting for me again—if there are still books and bookstores. Unless, of course, one hundred years from now zazen is common knowledge, an ordinary, daily part of the culture. Who knows how the text will be transmitted then? Interactive holography? Beams to the brain? In any case, I assume that *The Three Pillars* will be around in some form, nurturing and confusing readers, tormenting and inspiring them, still propping the gateless gate open for suffering beings—you and me.

That said, now for a bit of ancient history.

At a Rochester Zen Center sesshin about twenty years ago, someone sitting beside the altar near the front of the meditation hall (*zendo*) hears the dokusan bell *rrrrinnnngggg!* Instantly he swings around on the sitters' platform to rush out of the zendo and up the central stairs to dokusan. But *owwwwwwww!* That swinging turn is too wide and wild. His head hits the corner of the altar. Stunned, he is already flying forward, hand over the ear that took the blow. Then he stops. Blood covers the hand, dripping down the arm, pooling on the floor. He locates the zendo monitor, who is making the rounds with the kyosaku, and taps the monitor's shoulder from behind. The monitor turns, surprised. Then his eyes open truly wide. He grabs our friend, hauls him from the zendo to the kitchen, and lays him out on the kitchen floor. Blood drips and gathers.

A doctor who happens to be in the sesshin bandages the ear that has been pierced and torn by the altar. The injured sitter spends the next few hours in the monitors' room, out of sight of sesshin. That evening he retakes his place by the altar, and joins the next rush to dokusan. The hugely swathed and bandaged ear is never mentioned—not by him in dokusan, not by the roshi, not by the monitors who resume using the kyosaku as persistently on his shoulders as on anyone else's. If they were to miss the shoulder and accidently hit the bandaged ear, it might split. He has a fine sesshin, the pain of the ear keeping him steady and on beam even when others flag. To this day, a scar remains. It has a certain tenderness when rubbed.

Then there is the story of an old man and a tub, another tale from the past, maybe ten years ago. Roshi Kapleau had come to our house to use our Japanese bath, a big cedar tub in a converted side-porch. He liked the tub's spaciousness compared to the small Japanese bath at the Zen Center. I let him soak on his own, simply happy to have him under our roof. But I also stayed nearby, reading something or other, in case he needed anything.

That day I heard a call, loud and urgent, in the old man's familiar semi-hoarse, lower-belly voice: "Rafe! Rafe!"

"Yes, Roshi!" Dropping whatever I'm reading, I rush in—responsiveness is so very Zen.

He is straddling the tub, one foot still inside on the bench deep below the water, one foot out on the small stepladder, looking very discomfited. "My balls are hung up on the rim," he croaks. "I can't move! Help!"

"Old man, I've got you where I want you now," I think. "Your damn *Three Pillars* had me caught just like that for years. Say a word of Zen and I'll set you free." Well, I had my chance and blew it. I just said, "Sure, sure," and helped him down. When he was safely back on the tiled floor, I reminded him of Zen master Joshu, who once said, after taking a piss, "Even something as simple as this I must do for myself."

After Roshi was dressed, he and Rose and I sat on the couch and watched a video together. It was one of his favorites, and one of ours: *Casablanca*. What a movie! After Humphrey Bogart and Claude Rains walked companionably off into the fog, and the credits started to roll, we spontaneously exclaimed all together, "Play it again, Sam."

The same response arises with *The Three Pillars of Zen* every time I dip into it. It will remain a classic, a work not just for one time around. So play it again, Roshi. Play it again.

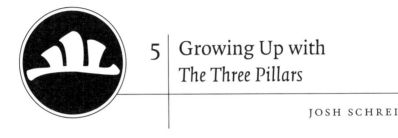

5 | Growing Up with The Three Pillars

JOSH SCHREI

W hen I was asked to contribute to a book on *The Three Pillars of Zen*, I felt a tangible excitement and a twinge of fear. *The Three Pillars* is the book that changed my parents' lives, that sent them to the Rochester Zen Center in 1969 to study under Philip Kapleau. My mother was twenty-one, with a freckled face and an intense gaze. My father, who refused on principle to go to Vietnam, had lived in Canada for some years. They ended up spending fifteen years at the Zen Center, most of the time as members of the resident staff. I was raised there, and consequently *The Three Pillars* shaped much of my early childhood.

For me, *The Three Pillars* was part of a worldview that was completely Buddhist. I remember being read excerpts from the book at a very young age. It seemed only natural when my parents taught me the proper meditation posture and techniques for following the breath. I had a huge poster of the Buddha in my room, facing me as I slept. I remember asking my mother what it meant to be a buddha, and puzzling over the laws of karma. At the tender age of seven or eight I was walking around mumbling, "Form is no other than emptiness, emptiness no other than form...."

The Center itself consisted of a very large urban house in a well-kempt, tree-lined neighborhood. Inside was a spacious *zendo* (meditation hall), and parts of the backyard resembled a Japanese garden. For kids, the Center was a huge playground with lots of rooms and walkways and decks to explore. The staff members were always ready to drop what they were doing and talk football with me, or roughhouse, or critique my crayon drawings of buddhas and superheroes. Sometimes I would run around to each room at the Center, visiting my friends: the kitchen staff, busy preparing bulgur and kasha and salads with sesame-seed dressing; the housekeepers in the basement, shaving curls of sweet yellow wax off the large temple candles; and the crazy guys in the woodshop, covered with sawdust. There was an increasing air of seriousness the closer one got to Roshi Kapleau's office and living quarters. I only entered Roshi's room once, with my friend Jake, when Roshi was away. We played cards on the floor. Dead silence surrounded us. I felt as if we were doing something really bad.

Now, some years later, I often reflect on my time at the Zen Center, and on my parents' decision to immerse themselves in Buddhism. I saw the search for enlightenment first-hand when it was in full swing. I saw the good aspects and the bad. I experienced the sincerity and the kindness of the people who undertook this search, and felt the sadness and the anger that still lived in some of them despite all the spiritual practice.

At times, I have been critical of Buddhism and have viewed the entire spiritual revolution in America with a large dose of skepticism. Nonetheless, I treasure the role that Buddhism has played in my life, and go back to its teachings for guidance and inspiration. So as I went down to the local bookstore to pick up a copy of *The Three Pillars*, I was not sure I wanted to unearth mixed feelings. I realized that I had not read the book since I was twelve years old.

It sat by my bed for several weeks, unopened. I would look at it from time to time, its shiny mint-green cover so different from the worn old hardcover that my parents used to own. I began to recall fragments and sentences from the book that I had absorbed in childhood. Something about oozing volcanoes of ego, swamps and jungles of delusion. Not a drop to be wasted. All beings without number, I vow to liberate.

SCHREI

When I finally picked the book up, it was a surprisingly quick read. I was reading something that was second nature to me, so familiar were the half-forgotten stories and phrases. The koan of Mu was first told to me when I was very young; I remember staying up nights mulling it over in my head. I can't count the number of times that I have repeated the four bodhisattva vows. I smiled to myself as I breezed through parables I knew like the back of my hand, and laughed a little at the book's complete dismissal of Hinayana Buddhism. The resounding descriptions of the *kyosaku* (encouragement stick) in action reminded me that on my fourth birthday I had been given a little kyosaku by a friend of my parents. On one side of the stick the words "Be kind to everyone" were written in black calligraphy. More memories leapt from the pages: a great flock of balloons magically released on the Buddha's birthday, a peaceful garden of gravel and rock, floors so polished they glistened. I could hear someone sharply striking a wooden mallet against a thick wooden board, and see the words written across that board: "Life is passing quickly by. Wake up! Wake up! Don't waste a moment!"

I never really knew Roshi Kapleau, but he was someone whom I respected. I understood that he was a great teacher, and even though at the time I didn't quite understand what made him wise, I knew that I should behave differently around him. If I was tearing around the Zen Center halls and realized that Roshi was nearby, I would slow down and straighten my posture. I saw that the adults also behaved differently when he was in the room. When Roshi was silent, they were silent. When Roshi laughed, everyone else laughed too.

I have a vivid memory of Roshi performing an ordination ceremony during a festival called Great Jukai. He was dressed in golden robes and a brocade shawl, holding a white horsehair whisk. It was shocking to see the two novice monks, whom I had known for years, sitting there totally bald. With conviction, Roshi ceremonially shaved off the final tufts of hair. There was a severity to the whole scene—the bells ringing, the stark whiteness of the newly shaven heads, the scraping sound of the razor. I felt odd, knowing that an important step had been taken but not really understanding what that step meant.

When Roshi gave a *teisho* (Dharma talk) at the Zen Center, all the Center kids and their young mothers would sit in a room in the basement and listen to the talk over a small beige speaker. I remember Roshi's voice, how he would clear his throat before speaking, how he would pause sometimes for a drink of water. The young moms listened

intently. It all seemed very important. I was often torn between my <figure></figure>
desire to play with the other kids and genuine curiosity about what
Roshi was saying.

The Three Pillars of Zen is strikingly different from the spirituality books
that are currently popular. With its fine-grained accounts of the ins and
outs of Zen practice and its heady philosophical commentary, it is difficult to imagine such a book being a best-seller today. Unlike the pop
spirituality books that promise seven easy steps to enlightenment, or
financial abundance, or a stable marriage, or whatever the flavor *du
jour* is, *The Three Pillars* is a straightforward, no-frills description of
Harada and Yasutani Roshis' brand of Zen practice. Reading it, one
gets a sense of the long, rich history of Zen, a sense of tradition that is
absent from much of what passes for spiritual literature today. The
questions asked are not "Do I have a soulmate?" or "Will my career pan
out the way I want it to?" but deep questions that strike to the heart of
the pain in all human beings. Why this cloudiness? Why this lack?
Why this suffering?

The fact that *The Three Pillars* sold so well when it first appeared is a
testament to the mindset of the times. In the late sixties and early seventies, people were thirsting for spiritual knowledge from the East, looking for a way to deal with the intense social and personal distress. In
many ways, it was also a more innocent time in America. I recall my parents' excitement at the prospect of realizing the true nature of mind, and
their firm conviction that enlightenment was within reach. There was a
sense that the world could be changed, that things were going to be different, that a new society could be created.

The very tone of *The Three Pillars* befits a book that was written at a
time of crisis. Philip Kapleau, as a court reporter at the World War II war
crimes trials, had seen more than his share of the misery and pain of the
world. Out of that anguish came questions, and out of those questions
came *The Three Pillars*. In the book, the enlightenment experience is presented to some degree as a cure for the neurosis and chaos of the times:

> Man, restless and anxious, lives a half-crazed existence because his
> mind...is turned topsy turvy. We need therefore to return to our orig-
> inal perfection and to wake up to our inherent purity and wholeness.

A ZEN CHILDHOOD While *The Three Pillars* goes into great detail about enlightenment, and chronicles many *kensho* (initial enlightenment) experiences, little is said of what one's life will be like after enlightenment. Grand claims are made: "When you truly realize the world of oneness, you could not fight another even if he wanted to kill you." Once enlightened, "you will feel the preciousness of each object in the universe, rejecting nothing, since things as well as people will be seen as essential aspects of yourself." These are beautiful descriptions, but it can be hard to translate them into the realities of day-to-day life. How does one go back to one's job after experiencing kensho? Or how does one raise a child?

The attitude of the young parents at the Zen Center seemed to be that all the years of Zen practice would pay off sooner or later, making them better parents in the end. A person who attained kensho would be more responsive to the needs of the children, able to truly provide love and clarity for the whole family. I remember my mother telling me at one point that she was meditating for my benefit, so that she could be a better mom, so that my world would be a little less crazy than the world in which she had grown up.

My parents and the other parents at the Zen Center did their best to create a loving environment for us children. There was an entire community, a Sangha, devoted to the same goals and principles. At its best, the Sangha was like a big extended family that included many friends and caring people. The ideas of nonviolence, compassion, and awareness were an integral part of our upbringing, and not just as ideas. There was a real sense of respect for the world and all creatures in it. Every summer we would go to Chapin Mill outside Rochester and release captive birds into the wilderness. I had the warm feeling that one gets when helping others. I felt good to know right from wrong. My friend Jake, another Sangha kid, would go out into the street after rainstorms so he could save earthworms from being stepped on.

This heightened moral concern was widely shared within the community. In this respect, I imagine that my childhood at the Center was similar to, say, a strict Catholic or Jewish upbringing. Every story I heard seemed to be a lesson: the kind rabbit who burned himself alive so that a poor stranger wouldn't starve, or the king who cut himself to bits to save a dove's life. Egolessness and selfless giving were extolled as the ultimate human virtues.

Growing Up with The Three Pillars

But my childhood also differed from a typical religious upbringing because Zen was a foreign tradition in America. The normalcy of the immediate neighborhood and the city of Rochester only sharpened the sense of how different we were. And, if anything, there was a feeling that we were better than everybody else. The rest of the world was trapped in a self-perpetuating cycle of ignorance, while the people at the Center were among the privileged few who knew a way out of this cycle. Ordinary everyday existence was a realm that needed to be transcended. Just out of reach was something else, something that, once attained, would make everything alright. In the meantime, before reaching that place, things were not OK.

The Zen Center was steeped in this sense of not-alrightness. I could feel it even as I ran from room to room or slid across the zendo floor in my socks. It stemmed from the belief that where we were at that moment, in America, in the world, in the twentieth century, was not enough. We were stuck in *samsara*, the endless cycle of suffering that had to be overcome. And so the people at the Center searched for the kensho that would deliver them from this not-alright world.

The expected transformation would come not through the attainment of something tangible like a good job or a house in the suburbs, but through something that seemed, at least to a child, very *in*tangible: the attainment of enlightenment. And even with all the meditation, there was no guarantee that we were ever going to get there! Occasionally I felt confused, wondering where all this searching was headed. How was everyone so sure that they could get to that promised place? How were they so confident that the way to get there was through Buddhist practice, and not through art, or writing, or friends, or dinner parties, or movies, or windsurfing? I remember wishing my parents would drop the whole enlightenment thing and just have fun for a change. But no one seemed interested in taking a break from the daily schedule of morning and evening meditation. Instead, we were going to be a better family through kensho.

It is easy to see how meditation can be very helpful as a *supplement* to modern family life. My family was unusual in that it was the *focus* of our life. It may be similar to the single-mindedness of parents who work all day and night so that their children can have a better future; paradoxically, they sometimes end up neglecting the very children they are trying to benefit.

One of the enlightenment accounts in *The Three Pillars of Zen* is telling in this regard. A very brief scene, easily missed, points out a quandary that *The Three Pillars*, and Buddhism in the West, has left unresolved. A Japanese executive, "Mr. K. Y.," who has been practicing Zen intently for eight years, is reading a book when a one-sentence quotation precipitates an enlightenment experience. Feeling ecstatic, the man exclaims to his wife, "In my present exhilarated frame of mind I could rise to the greatest heights!" His wife, laughing, replies, "Where would I be then?"

I see this question almost as a koan. It is not only a koan for those of my generation who grew up around Buddhist centers, but also for Western Buddhists in general. Now is an appropriate time to look at the effects that the search for enlightenment, conducted with utmost tenacity, has had on the families of those who undertook the search. More broadly, is it possible to integrate intense spiritual practice and the customary demands of family life? Many practitioners have risen to great heights, like K. Y. But in some cases, people who gave up everything to seek enlightenment left family and friends behind. Like the wife in the story, those who feel excluded ask, "Where does that leave us?" My father's parents never quite understood why he wanted to drop everything to join the Zen Center. Other parents of Zen Center staff were similarly upset. Many had survived the Depression and World War II to see their children, who were finally in a position to fully enjoy the American Dream, forsake the very underpinnings of that dream.

So, beneath the warmth and love at the Zen Center, beneath the bonds of community and the summons to transcendence, something else lurked. I only felt it clearly once or twice. It was sadness. Not everyone at the Zen Center had left family and friends to devote themselves to practice, or stepped off ladders that would lead to promising careers, but most had made some kind of sacrifice. Perhaps it was the sorrow one feels when, after fleeing from a mad world to a safe haven, one realizes that the world left behind, despite its madness, is indeed a world — powerful, enticing, and complete. Such a whole world cannot easily be replaced with daily meal chants or stately ceremonies or ancient Jataka tales. As the years passed, it became increasingly clear that the samsaric world would continue on without us, regardless of our renunciation, regardless of our kensho.

"SELECT A QUIET ROOM" A lot has happened in the thirty-year interval between the day my parents first picked up *The Three Pillars* and the day I bought my new copy. The search for enlightenment has cooled, or at least it is being expressed differently. A number of spiritual centers have suffered internal upheavals or scandals. Many people tried mightily for enlightenment but failed. Some practitioners had enlightenment experiences after years of effort, and then had to deal with the dismaying realization that the day-to-day problems of life remain. A few disciples stayed to pass on the lineage. Other long-time practitioners left disillusioned, wondering how to piece together new lives, their years of hard work and selfless service barely adding a line to a résumé.

I have noticed, in many of the original Zen Center staff members, a subtle movement over the years towards acceptance of their own humanity. Despite all the emphasis on attainment, they have become more comfortable with the notion that they will never be perfect. Irrespective of enlightenment, their lives will go on. It happened to my parents too, as if the direction of the wind had changed. Finally there was a sense that being right here, in samsara, on this planet, was alright after all.

Buddhism, still exotic but no longer so foreign, has continued to penetrate mainstream culture in unpredictable ways. Today, spiritual teachings from the East have increased dramatically in popularity, touching the lives of millions of people in America. Yet there is also more skepticism and cynicism about spirituality, which has become something of a fad. Pseudo-spirituality is widespread. Gone is the urgency of the sixties and of *The Three Pillars* itself, the sense that the whole world is going down and we better get enlightened quick. There is not the same excitement around the idea of enlightenment; though more and more people want spiritual teaching, they don't seem to have enlightenment as their final goal. Many of my generation have become cynical about the whole business, having had an overdose of Deepak Chopra on the best-seller list for the last three years. Even the Buddhists my age are not focused on the attainment of enlightenment the way the baby boomers were. This may be partly due to the cynicism my generation has towards *anything* that is forced upon us, be it pop music, politics, or spirituality.

Perhaps *The Three Pillars* is relevant now for different reasons than when it was first published. As our lives become more frenetic, Philip Kapleau's simple advice to "select a quiet room in which to sit" is increasingly necessary. In the sixties, the book introduced Westerners to the idea that they could awaken. Now, amid piles of spiritual schlock that promise material abundance and global consciousness shifts, the book's most important message may be that there is really no substitute for zazen. True spirituality involves direct experience of the nature of mind, and the first step in Zen is nothing fancier than following one's breath.

Since Shakyamuni's era, Buddhist teachings have made the long meandering journey from India to Tibet, Southeast Asia, China, Korea, Japan, and other countries. Each time that Buddhism came in contact with a new culture, it changed. With historical hindsight, many of those changes have come to seem natural, but they must have been difficult to foresee. American Buddhism is still in a fledgling state—who knows what form it will take? Whatever evolves, *The Three Pillars* will stand as a landmark in the history of Buddhism's migration to the West. And it should continue to inspire future generations, in new ways.

Shortly after reacquainting myself with *The Three Pillars*, I decided to do zazen for the first time in years. I lit a stick of incense and rolled up a towel to serve as a meditation cushion. I sat cross-legged on the polished wood floor in my bedroom. I kept my eyes downward, half-open. Slowly I began counting breaths. One on the inhalation, two on the exhalation, one on the next inhalation.... As thoughts arose, I did not pursue them, treating them as scattered clouds drifting across an otherwise clear sky. Of course, the clouds continued to drift: childhood memories of Rochester, conjectures about the future of Buddhism, my current relationship, the rent coming due.... But then the thoughts began to subside. It was just one person sitting. And yet it was not one person sitting alone, because people have been sitting in this way for twenty-five hundred years.

Growing Up with The Three Pillars

6 | The Authoritative Gaze

VICTORIA KIEBURTZ

M y first experience reading *The Three Pillars of Zen*, in 1984, was one of encountering an indomitable personality, more like being collared or shouted at than reading. It was equally an experience of intellectual and spiritual convergence. I had come from an ardently Christian household; my education from elementary school through college had been formally Catholic. However, for some years the daily practice of faith had been marked by inner questions and dissatisfaction. I felt impeded by the hierarchical, authoritarian structure of a church that seemed to preclude me, a layperson and a woman, from fully participating in its deepest mysteries. As this notion grew, so did my sense of being an outsider, with frustration focusing more and more on the role of the priest.

I see now that the alienating qualities I felt are not inherent in Christianity, any more than in other world religions. Separation and dissatisfaction are functions of the human condition. But this was the context in which I was presented with a copy of *The Three Pillars of Zen*, and may explain, in part, why the book captured my attention so completely and caused a nearly on-the-spot conversion to Zen practice.

Philip Kapleau's voice in *The Three Pillars* carries conviction almost to the point of zeal. His extensive introductions are marked by urgency, candor, and toughness. Once or twice there is even a touch of cockiness: "The full-lotus is naturally a harder nut to crack, but it no less will yield to a systematic effort." Kapleau makes bold claims, most notably that the practice of *zazen* (meditation) establishes "the optimum preconditions for looking into the heart-mind and discovering there the true nature of existence." For me, such declarations had the ring of truth and direct experience. The combination of zazen with the discovery of the true nature of existence was something of a revelation, bringing together religion (as the domain of faith and revealed truth) and the intense philosophical questioning I had been taught by the Jesuits in college.

The Three Pillars adroitly integrates theory, practice, and personal experience in a helpful, open-handed manner. Clear instructions are given in meditation practice; in fact, the reader is strongly encouraged to begin even without a teacher. In years since, Roshi Kapleau has said that one of his aims in writing the book was to allow those with no access to a teacher to benefit from Zen. This was certainly true for me. Because I had no background at all in Buddhism, I initially latched onto this aspect of the book, using it as a do-it-yourself manual. The subtle doctrines and the material about Zen as a religion were put on hold.

When I first read *The Three Pillars of Zen*, I was in Portland, Oregon, on a medical-student fellowship. Arriving back at the University of Rochester (my home institution), my future husband and I wasted no time in finding Philip Kapleau. We knew that we wanted to join the Zen Center, so we rented an apartment one block away. The first time we walked across to the Center, a blazing hot day in June, we found everyone outside in the parking lot holding a garage sale. A staff member whose shaved head was covered with a golf hat spoke with me about membership, and I poked around a bit. As I was turning to leave the grounds, I glanced inside the Center and saw Roshi Kapleau ascending some stairs. Nothing happened—he simply looked out at me. But the directness and intensity of Kapleau's gaze was unlike anything I had encountered.

Some days later I dreamed that I was scrubbing a floor on my hands and knees when someone walked up and stood looking down at me. I knew that it was him and was seized with a primal fear that if I looked directly at him I would die. I repeated to myself, "Don't look up, don't look up," like a mantra, as I scrubbed the floor. Then a fascination took

The Authoritative Gaze

hold of me and began to overtake the fear until…well, it was a dream. I looked up and awoke, like a shot fired out of a cannon.

Now, fifteen years later, I increasingly treasure *The Three Pillars* as a source book. The intervening years have brought numerous *sesshins* (meditation retreats) and daily work at the Zen Center, as well as the life dharmas of marriage, two children, and a part-time career in medicine. Regardless of changing circumstances, I find myself going back to certain sections of the book again and again, especially Bassui's Dharma talk and letters, Dogen's essay on being-time, and the commentary on the Ten Oxherding Pictures.

TRUST AND ATTUNEMENT   There is not as much written in Zen about the gaze of the teacher as there is in some other religions, such as Hinduism. In *The Spiritual Teachings of Ramana Maharshi*, a young boy gazes unreservedly at Ramana Maharshi for nearly thirty minutes, totally absorbed in the great saint's presence. This "silent" teaching, called *darshan*, is highly respected in Hinduism. I believe that it was the gaze of the teacher, literally and metaphorically, that first drew me to Zen and subsequently caused a radical reorientation of my sense of self.

A living teacher's literal gaze questions our assumptions and arouses faith and doubt in equal parts. A teacher's metaphorical gaze, as captured in books, reaches out in a social, historical context and illumines the scope of a spiritual tradition. It is within this gaze that we find the seat of authority in Zen. This authority is founded on the emptiness and presence of the teacher's mind, and the degree to which this emptiness reflects living truth.

My first reading of *The Three Pillars of Zen* had given me the impression that Buddhism was a nonauthoritarian religion, or at least a religion of decentralized authority in which the student could get away with the last word. Indeed, the book strongly emphasizes self-reliance and personal effort. The vivid portrayals of enlightenment experiences shatter any notion that practice is only for the sequestered renunciate. Each person already has what he or she needs to come to awakening. Enlightenment is our birthright—go for it! Although this is the absolute truth, it is not the whole truth.

Trust in the teacher, and full acceptance of the teacher's authority, are necessary for a student's movement from confusion to understanding. In a recent essay, a leading Japanese Zen master, Morinaga Soko

Roshi, writes movingly of his difficulty learning to trust his first teacher, Goto Zuigan Roshi. Zuigan had concluded their first interview by saying, "Zen training is impossible if you don't trust your teacher. Can you trust me?"[1] Coming out of a wartime experience in which he and his family had lost almost everything, and having seen former authorities branded as war criminals, Morinaga no longer knew what or whom to trust. I cannot cite the disruptions of a world war, yet the inability to trust has been there for me there as well. It comes partly from a deep intellectual skepticism, inculcated throughout the educational process. A Zen teacher asks us to drop many of our customary ideas and treasured assumptions, and that is painful.

At first, I tried consciously to diminish the teacher's relevance. Roshi Kapleau was not like an ordained Catholic priest, because he could not say Mass; he performed no comparable rituals that claimed to provide a mystical transformation beyond personal effort. And he was not like a university professor, because he was not offering a body of material to be mastered or challenged. In spite of my intuition in the dream, neither his presence nor his function struck me as transcendent. I concluded that the teacher would not have much of a role to play in my journey towards the absolute. This was a relief. Again, I find my own attitude echoed in the words of Morinaga, who doubted that he would be able to trust his first teacher:

> I thought to myself, "The world is full of imposters in high positions. How can he expect me to put my whole trust in him? I have only just met him. If it were that simple, I would have trusted someone or believed something before and need not have come here." However, the most important thing then was for me to be allowed to stay, even if it meant lying. So I said, "I trust you, please take me on."[2]

This very struggle is where the study of Buddhism commences. The teacher is not only at the heart of formal training; he or she is also a gateless gate to an entire world, the world in which all beings are perfect. As Zen master Dogen says in *The Three Pillars*, "One has to accept that in this world there are millions of objects and that each one is, respectively, the entire world." But passing through this gate comes at a price: surrender of the student's cherished sense of self. And the gaze, the relationship with the teacher that helps one accomplish this, was right there in *The Three Pillars* all along, clearly stated.

The Authoritative Gaze

I would like to relate an incident that brought this point home. It is in the spirit of Zen because a seemingly innocuous interchange revealed a world of truth and became a vehicle through which I experienced, in a new way, the nature of authority in Zen. Shortly after I joined the Rochester Zen Center, Roshi Kapleau retired and Sensei Bodhin Kjolhede succeeded him as director. Sensei Kjolhede has been my teacher since 1987. It is of him I now speak.

About a year ago I was planning to attend a sesshin, but I neglected to submit the required application. It wasn't until I saw the list of those accepted to sesshin that I realized, with a sinking stomach, that I had missed the deadline. I was working at the Center that day and went up to Sensei's office to explain. He must have been struck with an unconscious flippancy in my attitude because, to my surprise, he said with pointed carelessness, "Lucky for you, there is still room in the sesshin." He acted as if he might just as easily have said, "Oh, too bad for you, no more room in the sesshin."

His response made me angry. Here was the teacher with whom I had worked in *dokusan* (the private teacher-student encounter) twice a week for the past ten years, and on a daily basis as his clerical assistant for five. Yet he hardly seemed to care if I was in the sesshin and, worse, did not acknowledge how important sesshin is for me. I manage to attend one and a half sesshins a year and, because of scheduling difficulties, arrange them with my family six to eight months in advance. So I retorted hastily with a stiff laugh, "It is lucky for me! It is indeed!" and swept out of the room.

Just bravado. I actually felt miserable. It was as if I had tripped on a rock and fallen flat on my face, but in walking back and looking around, I couldn't see any rock; there was nothing there. What had I tripped on? Well, it turns out I had tripped on the whole universe.

Sensei probably thought that I assumed my presence in sesshin was more important than someone else's, and that someone would be bumped from the roster if necessary to make a place for me. Being on guard against the subtle designs of ego, he had bristled. Rules and procedures have a practical value; attention to them can be an expression of a student's mindfulness, and often her selflessness. My lack of attention to the deadline apparently sent up a red flag in his mind.

KIEBURTZ

Sufism, the mystical branch of Islam, has specific ground rules for the relationship between devotee and spiritual guide. After a devotee chooses a spiritual guide and opens himself to that person, his experience of Allah is, for a time, conditioned by the guide. Attunement between devotee and guide is essential to the devotee's broadening understanding. This kind of attunement is also essential in the work undertaken by a Zen student and his or her teacher. It is apparent throughout the enlightenment stories in *The Three Pillars of Zen*, especially in the account of "Mr. K. T.," the Japanese garden designer. After describing his fascination with Harada Roshi's voice, face, and overwhelming forcefulness, the designer relates an experience of unity with his teacher:

> Just in front of my knees I saw a large post and the leg of a small table overlapping. At that moment I felt the post to be the roshi and the small leg to be myself. Suddenly, this insight came to me: The post as a post is occupying all of heaven and earth, and the leg of the table as the leg of a table is doing the same. The roshi as roshi and I as I fill the entire cosmos.

The joy of that moment never left him, and he was never again afraid of the Roshi.

But what happens when attunement fails? A sincere student feels pain and works to get back in sync with the teacher. My reaction to Sensei's comment may seem overblown, but the strength of it exposes a central facet of the teacher-student relationship in Zen training. This relationship, like all phenomena, is ultimately empty and free of constraints, a living, dynamic expression of the deep truth that the student seeks. During periods of temporary blindness, the persistent intuition of this underlying truth sends the student into a tumult, casting about like a fish on a hook. In my case, the way out was to bow with a quiet, accepting mind and listen to what Sensei had to say. I decided that I would apologize the next morning in dokusan.

When I did, and he just nodded with a little furrow between his brows, I felt strange, as if I had never seen him before. Then, in a flash, I saw with fresh eyes that *I am the student*. It was wondrously simple. These roles were not confining but defining, the groundwork out of which truth unfolds. It seemed then that everything in the dokusan room was expressing the same teaching. I was surrounded. The lamp was a lamp; no amount of arguing or wishing would make it otherwise. Even if I smashed it in anger, it would still be something I couldn't argue with: a smashed lamp. The bell was a bell, the stick a stick. And later that day, as I was walking down the street, trees were trees and mailboxes mailboxes. They were exactly what they were, fully inhabiting themselves without apology or pause.

This is what Buddhists call suchness, not an elusive concept but an earthbound experience which teaches me that the ash tree is so high and the stones so hard and the air so cool and the suitcases so heavy. I think small children feel something of this sort when, two feet high with their arms thrown wide, they marvel at how "big" they are. Their bodies are *so big* because in that moment they feel both what they are and what they are not. They feel their exactness, their outline, their limit, and in doing so become huge, majestic, perfect.

Then it came home: this suchness is religious authority. This reality is what Zen teachers are pointing to, trying to get their students to see. This is the what Dante meant when he said, "The essence of this blessed state of being is to hold all our will within His will, whereby our wills are one and all agreeing." This blessed state is the all-agreeingness of the Buddha's awakening, the perfection that arises inseparably with the formless. I felt chastened and relieved of a great burden.

In the arena of spiritual training, Dante's image equally applies. If the student is able to hold all her will within the teacher's will, she is truly able to learn. Her fulfillment is gained by letting go of her concept of herself as authority and accepting a larger, more mysterious context of authority, one that is grounded outside her personal story, outside her wishes for acceptance and love. It is an authority that resides both in and through the teacher, physically embodying the reality of dependent coarising, in which phenomena arise conjointly. Teacher and student arise together and are dependently conditioned. Yet only when we fully accept this sitution do these same dependent conditions reveal their other face, empty and bottomless. Czeslaw Milosz writes:

> Love means to learn to look at yourself
> The way one looks at unfamiliar things,
> Because you are only one of many things.
> And someone who can look that way at himself
> Will heal his heart of many troubles.[3]

Zen takes this realization a step further. As Dogen says, "You think you are words and concepts, but you are mountains, rivers, grasses, and stones."

KIEBURTZ

When we look at what is unfamiliar, at whatever we regard as "other," we look upon our own face. In dealing with a Zen teacher, who has delved deeply into his own insubstantiality, one can expect, even without intellectual proof, that his reactions reflect truth. The real beauty is that even if the teacher's responses are off-base in the ordinary sense, it doesn't matter. As we adjust to the conditions the teacher presents—the stones that hurt our feet and the weeds that obscure the path—we are propelled through these conditions to the unconditioned. By bowing to the teacher, by accepting his viewpoint and fitting ourselves back into the parameters of his gaze, we become students in the broadest sense, free from confinement. In the end, ironically, we also free ourselves from the person of the teacher.

The teacher is not always conventionally "right." But as long as the relationship is based in trust, it becomes the context out of which truth unfolds. The student bows to the teacher, the teacher bows to truth, the student bows to truth. When the student bows to the teacher, she also accepts a set of boundaries within which all their interactions can unfold. Because the teacher's reaction to the student is generally free from self-concern, there can also be truth in *lack of* attunement. The mirror-like quality of the teacher's mind reflects back the student's defilements. If the student can see into an impasse, she will get a clear picture of the work that needs to be done, the distance she needs to travel in order to learn. As the student consciously turns the dial in an effort to pick up the teacher's frequency, they both begin to tune out their own static and mutually tune in to the great "it is so."

THE TEACHER-STUDENT RELATIONSHIP Why is the teacher so important in Zen? When we reexamine *The Three Pillars of Zen* in light of that question, we find a wealth of valuable material. After all, the very first of the three pillars is "teaching."

Throughout the book one feels Kapleau's receptivity to his own teachers. His deep respect and reverence for his immediate predecessors is especially obvious in his biographical notes on Harada Roshi and in the introduction to Yasutani Roshi's private encounters with Western students. Although an aim of the book is to provide a guide for Westerners who have no immediate access to a teacher, it in no way undercuts the value of teachers. In the introduction to Yasutani's lectures, Kapleau begins and ends with Zen master Dogen, highlighting the integral role played by Ju-ching, Dogen's own master. This introduction is a masterful interweaving of numerous teachers and ancestors, from Lama Govinda in the Tibetan tradition to Kapleau's own predecessors in Zen. Similarly, when we get to Yasutani's first lecture, we encounter Yasutani's words of praise for his own teacher, Harada Roshi.

This alternation between the perspectives of teacher and student continues throughout *The Three Pillars*. Kapleau is simultaneously teacher in relation to the reader, and student in relation to those presented in the text. Through him, numerous enlightened masters relate in concert to the practitioner. But without the clarity and strength of Kapleau's presentation, such transmission would not be possible.

In one of the enlightenment accounts, when an American schoolteacher first encounters Yasutani Roshi, she has a powerful reaction:

> When I saw the little man, seventy-seven yet bearing himself like fifty-seven, with the sparkling magnetism of youth in his eyes, all doubts vanished. "This is my master, for whom I was going to search all over India and Japan," I told myself, and was filled with a strange feeling of joy.

She goes on to call Yasutani the "greatest, whitest cloud I ever experienced." (His Zen name literally means "white cloud.") In such contexts, the teacher's gaze not only guides the student, it can transform the student's very notion of self. Jacques Lacan, the French psychoanalyst, writes correspondingly of the mother's gaze as forming the self of the child. Lacan realized that the small self (what we usually consider the self) is relational and impermanent, dependent on the attitude with which it is regarded. A difference is that the Zen teacher to whom the student opens her soul is not attached to any piece of the student's small self, and that difference has important implications. While a mother's gaze contains many attitudes and expectations besides love, a teacher's gaze is unfettered by expectation, essentially bottomless. It allows the student to drop through successive formulations of self into the open air, to begin to live freely.

As Roshi Kapleau has said, the Buddha Mind is like sound imprisoned on tape, or dry words entombed in sutras—the living force of an enlightened teacher is needed to recreate it. Sometimes the teacher is like a father, strict and reproving, sometimes like a mother, loving and comforting. In either case, an authentic teacher is a liberated personality, fluid and effortless in word and action, able to inspire students to experience life with the same immediacy. Such teachers reflect accurately what their students need. "To judge precisely at a glance—this is the everyday food and drink of a patch-robed monk." Although Kapleau gives newcomers to Zen the basic tools to get started, his aim is to lead them to a point where they recognize the need for a teacher.

The gaze of a Zen teacher is most palpably present in dokusan, the "eyeball-to-eyeball" encounter that figures so prominently in *The Three Pillars of Zen*. In dokusan, especially after days of meditation during a sesshin, one experiences an abatement of will, as if the self has no owner. This is when, as Kapleau says, the student becomes receptive to the teacher and the teacher's directions in a total way. In the same vein, during a formal Dharma talk (*teisho*), it can be as if the teacher's mind is amplified and his words are the only sound that ever existed. One contributor to *The Three Pillars* recalls the prelude to his awakening: "As the roshi spoke in a calm, quiet voice, I felt every one of his words filter into the deepest recesses of my mind." Shortly thereafter, the student had a breakthrough: "At last it dawned on me: *there is Nothing to realize!*"

These aspects of the teacher-student relationship have parallels in other traditions. For example, Sufism speaks of the disciple as a corpse in the hands of a washer, the guru. Interpreted in the proper spirit, this is an image of profound trust and tenderness. It is said of sincere Sufi disciples that "no capacity remains within them save to recall Allah; yea, not so much as the capacity to recall their own selves."[4] Nor to recall the teacher. It is only the burning desire for enlightenment that leads us to confront the teacher in this realm beyond self.

According to Buddhist doctrine, all concepts arise from the notion of "I," the assumption of self standing apart from other. In *The Three Pillars*, Kapleau says, "to renounce conception is to stand in darkness." The heart of formal Zen training is to renounce conception and stand in darkness in the presence of an "other," the teacher. This encounter also becomes the deepest source of confirmation, as so many of the enlightenment stories in *The Three Pillars* attest. The American ex-businessman, for instance, is flooded with mind-illuminating light while in the dokusan room. But the experience is not complete until his eyes and the roshi's eyes meet and "flow into each other"—and they burst out laughing together. Similarly, the Japanese executive rushes to see Yasutani Roshi the morning after an awakening, is unable to find words for his experience of emptiness, and finds himself crying uncontrollably in the master's lap. Yasutani's compassionate pat on his back during this episode is all the confirmation the student needs.

What did Kapleau know which led him to present Zen in this form? He knew, from his own experience, that only rigorous training, contingent on the authority of the teacher, provides the power needed to crush the ego. The ego, the part of ourselves that blocks us from spontaneously experiencing our own wholeness, is the principal source of our pain. It is the mind turned upside-down. It is delusive thinking and ignorance disguised as truth. I think of Banquo's words of caution after Macbeth was visited by the three hags who prophesied that Macbeth would someday be king:

> To win us to our harm, the instruments of darkness tell us truths, win
> us with honest trifles, to betray us in deepest consequence.[5]

Kapleau understands that these so-called truths and honest trifles are the wiles of ego, so *The Three Pillars of Zen* is a battle cry against the ego.

In this same spirit, Ramana Maharshi says:

> The ego is like a very powerful elephant which cannot be brought
> under control by any less powerful than a lion, which in this instance
> is no other than the guru, whose very look makes the elephant-like
> ego tremble and die. You will know in due time that your glory lies
> where you cease to exist. In order to gain that state, you should sur-
> render yourself. Then the master sees that you are in a fit state to
> receive guidance, and he guides you. [6]

The teachers presented to us in *The Three Pillars of Zen* are like lions. Their dignity, vigor, and potency permeate the text. Their palpable presence exposes the essential powerlessness of all ego and the insubstantiality of what we take ourselves to be.

There is no lack of authority in Buddhism. As Kapleau concludes, "In the person of a genuine roshi, able to expound the Buddha's Dharma with a conviction born of his own profound experience of truth, is to be found the embodiment of Zen's wisdom and authority." The acceptance of the teacher is fundamental to the effectiveness of the method, even as we recognize that the method is like a finger pointing to the moon. The moon is the unfathomable awareness of the Buddha. Kapleau knows how important that finger is, but he also knows that it is just a finger. That is why he offers us his teachers until we can find our own.

KIEBURTZ

Roshi Kapleau is old now, in his mid-eighties. After an active retirement, he has moved back to the Rochester Zen Center, to the quarters he vacated over a decade ago. Last year I stopped in to see him during the Center's holiday break. Word was that he had taken a bad fall coming out of his bedroom and knocked his head against a wall. I was eager to see how he was feeling. Entering his quarters, I checked the offending wall. Yes, there was a good-sized hole in it. Then, peeking around the corner, I encountered an unexpected sight: Sensei Kjolhede, arm in arm with Roshi, assisting him slowly towards the bed. It was naptime. When Roshi finally got seated on the side of the bed, he noticed me and smiled.

"I heard you took a fall," I said, continuing lightly, "Well, it's a good thing you have a hard head."

Roshi's smile widened. "Oh," he replied, as if relishing the opportunity, "I had another breakthrough."

The Authoritative Gaze

Philip Kapleau, Shunryu Suzuki, and Thich Nhat Hanh

7

ARNOLD KOTLER

I n December 1969, when I was twenty-three, I took a leave of absence from the University of California at Berkeley to consider how to proceed with my life. It was a time of ferment nationwide, and I needed to sort out what was most important. I had recently become interested in Zen, so I purchased a copy of *The Three Pillars of Zen* and received instruction in *zazen* (sitting meditation) at the Berkeley Zen Center. Then I decided to hitchhike north in search of a spiritual community.

My first stop was a small commune in southern Oregon, where I spent hours sitting zazen and reading *The Three Pillars of Zen* by candlelight. At that time *The Three Pillars* was the only book on Zen practice in English. Philip Kapleau's emphasis on concentration, effort, and attainment provided a clear and encouraging way to proceed. After a week or so, I continued traveling north. On Quadra Island, British Columbia, I happened to meet a man who had just returned from Tassajara Zen Mountain Center near Big Sur, California; Tassajara was (and is) part of the San Francisco Zen Center. He advised me to return to San Francisco and practice under the guidance of Shunryu Suzuki

Roshi. So, after just three weeks of pilgrimage, I hitchhiked back to the Bay Area and went to the San Francisco Zen Center. The moment I walked through the door, I knew I had found my true home.

A month later, I sat my first *sesshin*, a week-long intensive meditation retreat. Sesshin literally means "to gather the mind." On the fifth day, I felt myself having a breakthrough that seemed to be similar to the *satori* experiences described in *The Three Pillars of Zen*. I sat on my cushion, clenched my teeth, tightened all the muscles on my face, and felt waves of nausea traversing through me. I was sure this was "It." So I asked to see one of the teachers, Dainin Katagiri Roshi, to tell him of my extraordinary accomplishment.

Waiting outside the *dokusan* (interview) room, I thought about the laudatory response the teacher would give me when I told him what had happened. The bell from the teacher's room rang. I stood up, bowed from the waist at the door, bowed again inside the door, did three full prostrations, sat down, and told Katagiri about my experience. He looked at me deeply and finally said, "Not so good. Please go take a warm bath and rest for a while."

I share this account of my "breakthrough" not to suggest that striving for satori is an invalid way to practice, but to illustrate how such striving can lead to unfruitful results without proper guidance.

Later that same year, 1970, *Zen Mind, Beginner's Mind* by Shunryu Suzuki came out. In the book and in his teaching, Suzuki Roshi used every opportunity to de-emphasize enlightenment. He even poked fun at those seeking to attain it. In response to one student's question, he said, "What makes you think I'm enlightened?" To another he said, "If you experience enlightenment, you might not like it." He encouraged us to practice *shikantaza* (serene sitting), brought from China to Japan by Zen master Dogen in the thirteenth century.

Though the effects of practice vary from one person to another, it is possible to generalize about the strengths and the weaknesses of various approaches. The strictness of Rinzai-style Zen seems to bring about rock-like stability and intense energy, yet if the admonition to "sit through the pain" is taken too far, it can cause some meditators to injure themselves (mostly knees and backs). I have also noticed an excessive solemnity at some Zen centers in Europe and North America.

Soto-style Zen, as taught in America by Suzuki Roshi and others, offers clear instruction in posture and breathing: count inhalations and exhalations, follow the breath without counting, or do shikantakza. At

Philip Kapleau, Shunryu Suzuki, and Thich Nhat Hanh

the end of each sesshin, Suzuki Roshi would remind us that the most important meditation period had not occurred during the week just completed; rather, it was the meditation period the following morning. Through shikantaza, dedicated students at the San Francisco Zen Center have developed calmness, steadfastness, and deep concentration. Still, some people feel that Soto-style Zen does not offer enough explicit guidance on how to practice outside the meditation hall. Although Suzuki Roshi emphasized practicing the spirit of zazen all day long, this encouragement may be too subtle and indirect for many of us.

After Suzuki Roshi's death in 1972, I continued training under the guidance of his successor, Richard Baker Roshi, and appreciated those years very much. Then, in 1984, after fifteen years at the San Francisco Zen Center, I began to study with Thich Nhat Hanh, a Vietnamese Zen master. Since his forced exile from Vietnam, Thich Nhat Hanh has led a community of practitioners, called Plum Village, in France. In his teaching he emphasizes mindfulness of our body, feelings, mind, and environment throughout daily life. His students call him Thây (pronounced "tie"), a Vietnamese term of respect for a teacher or a monk.

One hot July day, I was sitting in the meditation hall at Plum Village, struggling to stay alert. I noticed that several friends were falling asleep. Then I saw Thây quietly walk up to the drowsy meditators, remove his cone-shaped straw hat, and offer a cool breeze by using his hat as a fan. What a contrast to the *kyosaku*, the stick used to wake up those who dozed at Tassajara!

Thich Nhat Hanh has touched thousands of people by his compassion, forged in the suffering of Vietnam, and by his capacity to express the teachings of Buddhism in a straightforward yet poetic way. He has done much to develop concrete practices of mindfulness that we can use in our daily lives. An example is telephone meditation: take three conscious breaths while the phone rings to calm yourself and be fully present before answering.

Years ago, Thich Nhat Hanh made the decision to take each step slowly and in mindfulness. Walking meditation, especially outdoors, has since become a primary practice for many. Thây encourages us to be gentle with ourselves: "go slowly, breathe, and smile." In time, this approach brings joy and a degree of peace. Still, I must admit that some of us who practice with Thây overemphasize the lightness of being and fail to develop real meditative concentration. Thich Nhat Hanh's charisma and excellent character are inspiring, yet again there is a caveat: the tendency to place the teacher on a pedestal can inhibit us from cultivating our own intelligence about practice.

In Zen, for beginners especially, the line between practice and non-practice is often too sharply drawn. We practice well while sitting on our cushions, but we are not especially mindful in our daily lives or serious about issues of moral conduct. Upheavals at many American Zen centers have shown how hard it is to follow the basic precepts of not harming others. One day at Plum Village, after hearing news of a crisis in another Zen community, Thich Nhat Hanh said to me, "I guess Zen Buddhism doesn't work." It was a rather provocative statement, but he didn't elaborate. Ten days later, he continued the conversation: "...if you don't practice correctly."

There are many valid ways to practice the Buddha's Way. Granted, it is of great value to stay with one practice deeply and not shop around too much. For this reason, Roshi Kapleau rarely gave his students permission to study with other teachers. Yet if we practice intelligently, with mutual respect and acceptance, we can profit from the many good teachers and centers that are available.

The approaches of these "three pillars of Zen"—Philip Kapleau, Shunryu Suzuki, and Thich Nhat Hanh—complement one another and provide the essential elements of a well-rounded Zen education. The names of Taizan Maezumi Roshi, Robert Aitken Roshi, and so many other great teachers and their disciples can also be added to the list. It is wonderful that we are becoming more familiar with the strengths and weaknesses of the different streams of Zen and other Buddhist traditions. We can practice more skillfully if we understand which aspects our own lineage emphasizes. And we can benefit from exposure to other forms of practice even while we train primarily in the way best suited to our spiritual needs and temperament.

I bow deeply to all my teachers: to Roshi Philip Kapleau, as my first Zen teacher through his writings, and as a great ancestor to all of us who are practicing Buddhism in the West; to Shunryu Suzuki Roshi, a beacon of Zen; to Richard Baker Roshi, from whom I continue to learn; and to Venerable Thich Nhat Hanh, with whom I have been walking the path of mindful living.

Philip Kapleau, Shunryu Suzuki, and Thich Nhat Hanh

8 | Many Paths, One Path

ALAN SENAUKE

Last night Philip Kapleau appeared to me in a dream. In waking life we have never met. A thin, angular, aging man came through a door and strode past me down a sunlit hallway. Walking by, he turned slightly and, addressing me softly, personally, asked how my work with the tribal Buddhists in Bangladesh was going. I was surprised to see Roshi Kapleau, and even more surprised that he knew about our modest Buddhist Peace Fellowship work in a distant corner of the world. Though he has long supported engaged Buddhism, it touched me deeply that he was really paying attention to what we were doing. Roshi Kapleau was down the hall and through another door before I could regain my mental balance and ask about his own delicate health.

Early Monday mornings at the Berkeley Zen Center, where I live, a Zen student gives what we call a "Way-seeking-mind talk" — the story of what brought that person to the *zendo* (meditation hall). It is a kind of autobiography without rules. Each of us tells our own story as it appears to us at that moment. None is quite true. This is one version of mine.

Strands twine together into strong threads that make a whole cloth of life: an intuitive taste since boyhood for the unadorned; left-leaning politics that honor the actions and voices of ordinary people; the search for a plain and miraculous written language; traditional folk music; and Zen. From the vantage point of the present, I can see the various pieces of my life making the cloth whole, though there were long years when I seemed to wander in despair. Then I had to go on instinct, trying different paths, stepping back out of blind alleys.

In high school I was drawn to the Chinese and Japanese literature I read in translation. Basho's *Narrow Road to the Deep North* had more appeal than Kerouac's *On the Road*. Basho offered plainness and lightness and humor, with less self-concerned drama. Similar notes were struck by the great T'ang-dynasty poets like Wang Wei, Su Tung-p'o, and my favorite, Han-Shan or "Cold Mountain," who at moments reminded me of William Carlos Williams. In college I studied with the poet Kenneth Koch. We were working at a kind of language that was spontaneous, playful, open to the wide world, and sensitive to the infinite mysteries that shine through everyday speech and events.

The copy of *The Three Pillars of Zen* on my desk is inscribed "July 1968." It is a third printing, issued in April of 1968, the month that Martin Luther King was murdered. That same April, I was among a group of student protesters who took over buildings at Columbia University. After living for a week in the university president's office, we were arrested. Amid all this tumult, *The Three Pillars of Zen* opened the door to Zen practice for me. The Zen books I had read—poetry and literature, Alan Watts and D. T. Suzuki—had said almost nothing about the actual practice of Zen. Yasutani Roshi's lectures and other parts of the book finally explained *how to do it*. This was and is the priceless gift of Roshi Kapleau's elegantly constructed work. How many Zen students have drawn first inspiration from this well?

At the time, I was also exploring the wild and crooked way of psychedelic drugs. Beginning in December of 1966, a handful of us regularly used marijuana, LSD, mescaline, and other substances (including such oddities as baby Hawaiian woodroses and baked banana skins) to explore the boundaries of consciousness. Mostly we did this in New York City, sometimes riding the subways to go hear music or visit friends similarly engaged. I would test myself to see how stoned I could be and still keep it together.

On a trip to Binghamton, New York, visiting an old high school friend at Harpur College, I first heard about the Rochester Zen Center. One of my friend's roommates was starting to do *zazen* (meditation) there.

Many Paths, One Path

Though I was not ready to go to Rochester, just knowing that there was a place nearby where one could practice planted a seed.

In the early summer of 1968, my friends and I were passing time in New York waiting to learn the disposition of the court cases coming out of the Columbia occupation. It was terribly hot. We were crowded into my friend's aunt's Upper West Side apartment, doing temporary work and writing outlandish stories for pay, articles which were published in the *Star Chronicle*, a tabloid. We were dying to get out of New York and head for California. Eventually, about eight or ten of us made it to Berkeley in driveaway cars and bargain-rate airplanes. We found a sublet apartment on Benvenue, near the Berkeley campus, and embarked upon some sixties-style California adventures: psychedelic music, the requisite chemicals, hitchhiking to Big Sur, martial law in the Berkeley streets (during the People's Park controversy), and of course Zen.

Yasutani Roshi's lectures on Zen training in *The Three Pillars of Zen*, along with the book's illustrated postures, had given me a notion of where to start. At home in New York, I had tried to sit on pillows and count breaths. But my legs hurt and my concentration was weak. I was intimidated by the pain, unable to open to it. My back did not want to stay upright. The wall before me, seen through half-opened eyes, swam with colors. I half hoped that these images were *makyo*, the illusory visions that other sitters reported, but more likely the sensations were just the blood spinning through narrow capillaries in the back of my eyes.

There was another difficulty, something I am still working with thirty years later. The moving accounts of contemporary enlightenment experiences, as well as Yasutani's interviews with Westerners, were simultaneously encouraging and off-putting. Enlightenment is at the center of *The Three Pillars* in a way that sets it apart from almost all of the English-language Zen books that followed it. It was clear that these interviews were the authentic testimony of ordinary people who had single-mindedly applied themselves to practice under the guidance of a master. But, in the midst of the Vietnam War and the harsh realities of racism, people my age were radically questioning authority and our place in society. Growing up in the fifties and sixties, we had been channeled down a path of achievement and materialism laid out by parents and teachers who had come of age in the Depression years. Bob Dylan spoke for us when he said, "Don't follow leaders. Watch the parking meters." I had had enough of goals and accomplishments in school, and I was reluctant to strive for anything else, including "*satori*."

SENAUKE

In Berkeley, I found the Zen center that Sojun Mel Weitsman had established on Dwight Way a year earlier, at the suggestion of Shunryu Suzuki Roshi. Our small circle of New York poets and activists regularly climbed the narrow stairway to the bare-wood attic zendo on Dwight Way. The space was well loved and meticulously tended. Mel's open-minded and attentive spirit included everyone who wished to meditate. We did zazen around the room under the slanting roof. Because the chanting was entirely in Japanese, we read the clipped and rhythmic syllables of the *Maka Hannya Haramita Shingyo* (*Heart of Perfect Wisdom Sutra*) from worn yellow chant cards. It was strange, but I persevered.

For better or worse, the regular members had an attitude of studied coolness to newcomers. I had the idea from my little reading that despite an emphasis on transcendent ordinariness, Zen and Zen people were somewhat austere. It certainly seemed that way at the time, and even today one hears similar complaints. Of course, this feeling of others' aloofness was closely tied to my own lack of confidence and the slowly unfolding process of identity formation. The upshot was that in the summer of 1968 I came and went without talking to people at the Berkeley Zen Center, and without them talking to me.

The silence might have helped me to find my own place. Now I think I would know how to use it. But back then, it kept me from asking important questions about the practice, from learning that Suzuki Roshi's and Mel Weitsman's style of Zen was significantly different from the style of Zen presented by Philip Kapleau and his Japanese teachers.

As I read *The Three Pillars* now, I am struck by the book's assurance that *kensho*, or satori, is attainable. I am especially moved by the letters of Yaeko Iwasaki, an inspired but chronically ill Japanese woman of twenty-five who died just after "grasping the tail of the ox." Her realization is movingly confirmed by Harada Roshi. She herself came to Zen when her father, stricken with fear by a heart condition, began practicing with Harada Roshi. In 1968, when I was twenty, this material was all too dramatic and remote for me to reckon with. Now I know in my own body that death and realization are both unpredictable and surprisingly near. The urgency of Yaeko Iwasaki's practice, of Philip Kapleau's, and of my own is clear to me.

There are stories that suggest that Yasutani Roshi and Nakagawa Soen Roshi (another influential master) looked somewhat askance at the Soto Zen that Suzuki Roshi was planting in the Bay Area. They apparently felt that Zen students in San Francisco and Berkeley were not properly pushed to develop single-minded intensity. The practice did not have enough rigor or energy. In *The Three Pillars*, Yasutani declares, "If you are truly doing *shikantaza* (just sitting), in half an hour you will be sweating in an unheated room, because of the heat generated by this intense concentration."

In comparison, Sojun Weitsman recently wrote the following about Suzuki Roshi's practice of shikantaza:

> Suzuki Roshi's simple day-to-day activities—the way he would sit down and stand up, eat his dinner, walk, put on his sandals—this was his expression of shikantaza. Everyday activity with no selfishness— just doing the thing for the thing — that was his shikantaza. We usu- ally say that shikantaza means "just sitting." And that's true.... But this "just" has a special meaning. It means "without going any fur- ther" or "without adding anything extra."

Are Suzuki's and Yasutani's versions of shikantaza as different as they sound? Is either approach what Zen master Dogen meant by "think not-thinking," in his treatise "Rules for Zazen"?[1] Unless one knows practice intimately, such comparisons can be misleading. Both methods are thoroughly radical in their own way. We can be certain that each Zen master offered his heart's path to awakening. I lean in Suzuki Roshi's direction, but I honor the paths not taken.

The preeminent figure in Suzuki Roshi's lineage is Dogen, the great thirteenth-century master. Dogen's words, woven throughout *The Three Pillars*, got my attention even thirty years ago. As a beginner I couldn't know that Dogen's writings were not yet available in English outside of scholarly journals. The difficult selection from "Being-time" that Kapleau translates was beyond me then, but I was encouraged by the way Dogen's *Treasury of the True Dharma Eye* (*Shobogenzo*) seemed to reinforce my intuitions about the interpenetration of transcendent and ordinary. That summer in Berkeley I wrote Zen-inspired poems—best forgotten now—lifting phrases from Dogen, phrases I could resonate with but not understand.

At summer's end in 1968, I returned to New York and my last year of college at Columbia. Apart from good intentions, I carried the tools of my first Zen efforts. My friends and I brought back *zafus* (sitting cush- ions) and *zabutons* (mats), and when the fall term began I registered for an introductory Japanese class. From my reading of the Beats and of Kapleau, I imagined that I had to go to Japan, as they had, to do real

SENAUKE

Zen. However, in the face of political and personal turmoil, I set the practice aside for many years. I sensed that there was something missing in my limited understanding, but I did not know what it was.

THE BONDS OF SANGHA   Until serendipitously returning to Berkeley in 1982, I spent much of the next fifteen years in a search for something I have now found—community, or what Buddhists call Sangha. Rereading *The Three Pillars of Zen*, I find few words about Sangha or the act of taking refuge in the Three Treasures, one of which is Sangha. Roshi Kapleau's focus was elsewhere, and my own immaturity kept me from appreciating the role of community in Buddhist practice. Wrestling with issues of loneliness, private preference, collective responsibility, privilege, communal living, and political action, I sought clarity, but more often than not I met my own suffering. Later I came to understand how central Sangha and refuge are to Suzuki Roshi's teaching. He and his students acted in this spirit when they started the San Francisco Zen Center and created the first Westernized Zen monastery at Tassajara. Mel Weitsman's teaching has similarly had Sangha at its root, even in the early days. Today I feel deeply grateful for the life and family that have come to me through the years I have been in Berkeley.

Having taken a priest's vows, I have a sense of Sangha that extends beyond the ritual circle of ordination. In this country, Buddhist community is built on the collective practice, effort, attention, and support of everyone involved, whether lay or ordained. Although few will choose the monastic path as traditionally conceived, there are many ways to explore the spirit of that path in contemporary life. In fact, the material excesses and sensual temptations of late-twentieth-century America give renunciation and relinquishment new meanings unimagined by our monastic ancestors. The bonds of Sangha strengthen us in these efforts, enabling us to be whole as we let go of deep habits of self-centeredness. In *The Three Pillars of Zen*, Bassui and others tell us that bowing to the buddhas is "a way of horizontalizing the mast of ego in order to realize the Buddha-nature." This bowing, actual or metaphorical, can be extended to our Sangha comrades and ultimately to all beings. I keep finding new ways to horizontalize the mast of ego at the Berkeley Zen Center and in the community of engaged Buddhists involved in the Buddhist Peace Fellowship, where Sangha is built through social action that reaches out to the wider world.

Many Paths, One Path

I wonder what Roshi Kapleau would have said if he had written *The Three Pillars of Zen* in America rather than in Japan. Who could have imagined that the book—and Kapleau's return to the United States—would be perfectly timed to hit the spiritual revolution of the late sixties? Settling in Rochester, Kapleau soon created a large and vital community that served as one of the motors of Zen in this country. It continues to be so. I know that there have been difficulties in Rochester, as there have been in San Francisco and elsewhere. In America we are always trying to find the point of balance between authority and equality. Our communities sometimes draw strange, suffering individuals. Living in close proximity has always been hard, and practice is demanding. The Buddha's myriad precepts for monks testify to these difficulties, as do the detailed regulations of Japanese monasteries. But in Rochester and elsewhere, as Zen and other Buddhist sects find their way in the West, new models of Sangha are developing. I suspect that if Roshi Kapleau had written *The Three Pillars* after a few years in Rochester, he would have said more about the refining challenges of living with one's Dharma brothers and sisters, and one's teacher.

As a priest (actually, a strange kind of semi-renunciate monk with wife and kids and a job), my main vow is to liberate sentient beings. One interpretation of that vow is to make the practice available and accessible to all. So the link with engaged Buddhism is clear. In my work for the Buddhist Peace Fellowship, I try to carry this notion of practice and true liberation into the messy, ambiguous realms of social and political action. This work is, I believe, consonant with the responsibilities Philip Kapleau assumed when he wrote *The Three Pillars* and took the difficult next step of creating communities of practice in the world.

Although *The Three Pillars* demonstrates that Philip Kapleau is deeply indebted to his own Zen teachers, I am surprised to find little explicit discussion of the need to find a good teacher. It is difficult, maybe impossible, to keep oneself on the path through solitary practice, particularly in the case of Zen, which contains teachings and cultural elements that turn our habits on their heads. Going to a teacher, whether for koan training or practice instruction, is a necessary act. It is also an act of submission, intimately related to the task of shaking off self-centeredness. To accept the guidance of a teacher is probably hard for people everywhere, and it is especially hard for Westerners. Yet to live and work with a person who has completely given her or his life to Dharma is a rare and wonderful opportunity. You see how the teacher moves, how he treats people and things, how he is human and fallible and even exasperating, how he is always capable of returning to the present. Daily contact with my own teacher, Mel Weitsman, has been one of the great gifts of living at the Berkeley Zen Center. In this intimate way a teacher helps a student inhabit his or her own life fully.

Kapleau himself had extraordinary teachers in Harada and Yasutani. Late in Yasutani Roshi's career, he made periodic trips to Hawaii and the States, but the opportunity to do *sesshin* (retreat) with him was quite special. Three of our main Zen teachers here in America—Robert Aitken, Taizan Maezumi, and Kapleau himself—have come directly from this line of practice. Each of them, I think, would insist on the necessity of refining and personalizing one's practice with the help of a teacher. I imagine that when *The Three Pillars* was published, Kapleau did not yet presume to see himself as a Zen teacher. But by the time of his later book, *Zen: Merging of the East and West*, he found much to say about the vital relationship of teacher and student, informed by his experience in Rochester.

My appreciation for Roshi Kapleau and for *The Three Pillars of Zen* runs very deep. A life of Zen calls for dedication and rededication at all the hard places. I value his emphasis on the fundamentals of practice, and admire the personal way he has worked to adapt those fundamentals to our own strange and sometimes thickheaded American needs. I also appreciate his upright sense of morality and his principled care for the wide world. These themes emerge even more clearly in his later books. His example and concern have meant a lot to me over the years.

The work of Zen and the work of socially engaged Buddhism are not different. The basic struggle is about liberation, something Philip Kapleau speaks of again and again. Engaged Buddhism was instinctual for me at first; now, after nearly a decade as director of the Buddhist Peace Fellowship, it is a continuously expanding field of inquiry and a personal mission. My experience is one of constant motion, from inner practice to outer practice and back again. The Zen handed down (or across) from Suzuki Roshi to my root teacher Sojun Weitsman and then to me celebrates all of these strands as "ordinary mind." In time, the barriers and distinctions between inner and outer fall away, yet as long as we live in our world and in our bodies we must attend to both. Presenting our true mind, being present with our partners, children, and co-workers, living in Sangha, feeding the hungry, ending war—this is Zen practice.

Many Paths, One Path

Those who come to us in dreams have an intimate place in our mind. Roshi Kapleau's appearance in my dream speaks of my gratitude to him. And I am heartened by the feeling that he was acknowledging me and my work. I only got a glimpse of him, but a glimpse was enough. I saw a man, a teacher, a guide who knew how to pay attention even in someone else's dream. All through my life, guides have stepped forth in vivid dreams. Some have been close and familiar. Others, like Philip Kapleau, I still hope to meet face to face.

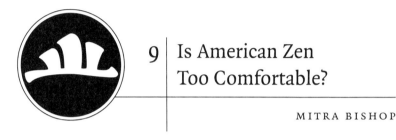

9 | Is American Zen
Too Comfortable?

MITRA BISHOP

T he *Three Pillars of Zen* was not the first book on Zen that
I read, but the second—only because it was not available in
Turkey at the time. Although I did not read it until I had already
begun doing *zazen* (meditation), that practice of zazen was taught to me
by someone who had read *The Three Pillars* and was following its
instructions.

It was in Turkey that my life had disintegrated in every way; suddenly I was a woman alone far from home, and a failure to boot. Though
there were no Zen groups in Istanbul, amazingly I met a Turkish man,
Ergun, who was a member of the Rochester Zen Center. "Zen"—
people had little idea what that meant—was a topic of some interest
among the educated Turks, yet Ergun and an American military man
stationed near Istanbul seemed to be the only people actually practicing
zazen. Everyone else was caught up in the heady, seductive pursuit of
an affluent lifestyle, newly available in the Turkey of the 1970s. Not until
one has grown weary of trying to assuage inner emptiness or sadness
with material possessions or other stopgap measures is one open to the
potential of zazen. On that score, I was ready.

Ergun said, "I can show you how to do zazen, but you also need to read *The Three Pillars*." For two years of solo practice, the book sufficed as teacher and Sangha (community). Then I felt the need for a structured practice environment and the companionship of fellow practitioners. So in 1976 I traveled back to the States to Rochester, home of the book's author. *The Three Pillars of Zen* went with me, by now well worn from frequent reading.

Unfortunately, in Rochester I measured each nuance of practice against the book. "Aaah! Enlightenment is about to strike!" Of course it couldn't possibly strike with all my weighing and measuring. The book's accounts of *kensho* (enlightenment) experiences were a double-edged sword. On the one hand, they kept me going when practice was difficult. The inspiring stories had fulfilled this role especially in Turkey, where there was no one to talk to about practice, no teacher to encourage me on the path. On the other hand, they were a too-handy and ultimately false road map; as long as I clung to the experiences of others, my practice remained superficial. The book speaks of a "map . . . charting [one's] entire spiritual journey," but that claim can be misleading. Some guidance along the way is crucial, and a look at the mistakes others have made is especially helpful. However, a map charting one's entire spiritual journey, if such a thing were possible, would be a distraction and a hindrance.

After sixteen years of training in Rochester, I again sensed that it was time to make a change, and decided to go on a pilgrimage, an ancient Buddhist tradition. Having previously lived in Burma and Thailand, and with too little money to do much traveling, I aimed for Japan. There I spent two months at Sogenji, a Rinzai Zen temple in Okayama, followed by some time in Kyoto, sitting at Daishu-in, a subtemple of the famous Ryoanji temple. I also went north to Obama to attend a week-long *sesshin* (meditation retreat) with Tangen Roshi, who had taken Philip Kapleau under his wing while they were both training at Hosshinji. Tangen Roshi now heads his own temple, a stone's throw from Hosshinji. Before I left Japan, I knew that I must return. The following September I went back and stayed for three years, until the spring of 1996.

By joining the community of resident practitioners at Sogenji, a temple that upholds monastic-style training, I was able to throw myself into an intensive practice environment that was both very familiar and very unfamiliar. In the process, I came to see aspects of American Zen in sharper outline, and gained a deeper appreciation of the complexities inherent in Zen's transmission to the West. My time in Japan also prompted further reflections on *The Three Pillars of Zen*.

Traditionally, little or no instruction is given to beginners in Zen temples in Japan, and certainly none by a roshi. In Rinzai monasteries, Zen master Hakuin's "Rohatsu Exhortation," which contains some instruction on breathing practice and basic elements of posture, is read during the Rohatsu sesshin (the year's toughest retreat, in December), but only then. In their willingness to offer instruction, Yasutani Roshi and Harada Roshi, the two principal teachers in *The Three Pillars*, seem to have been exceptions. Even *dokusan* or *sanzen*, the private encounter with the teacher, is generally not allowed until one has clearly and for a prolonged period demonstrated an earnest vow to continue practice despite all obstacles. After repeated entreaties, a Japanese friend of mine was finally permitted to come to daily sittings at Sogenji. Then, even though she attended every possible moment of every possible sesshin (and held down a job at the same time), it was more than a year before she was allowed a private meeting with the roshi.

There are books in Japanese that teach the full- and half-lotus sitting postures and temple protocol for monks: how to wear the robes, do the prostrations, unwrap one's bowls at mealtime, and so on. And there are a few English translations of advice for beginners by distinguished roshis, such as Yamada Mumon's *How to Practice Zazen*. But none of these works have the substance or breadth of *The Three Pillars of Zen*. Philip Kapleau's book was—and is—a landmark in any language.

The traditional method of entering a Rinzai Zen monastery is to arrive in the entrance foyer, bow deeply, and beg acceptance, forehead literally down on the steps. Rebuffed for days, one remains in that position until allowed (perhaps) into a small room secluded from the normal routine. There one is expected to demonstrate one's ardor for practice by engaging in zazen day and night. If that hurdle is passed, one may be allowed to join in the daily practice, at the very bottom of the totem pole. Even then, there is little of the sort of guidance that Westerners expect. Rather, foreigners and Japanese alike are met with one obstacle after another. Keep your mouth shut and figure it out for yourself—this is the traditional way. "Nowhere in Japan will you find Zen teaching set forth so thoroughly and succinctly, so well suited to the temper of the modern mind, as at [Harada Roshi's] monastery," *The Three Pillars* asserts. Indeed.

Is American Zen Too Comfortable?

At Sogenji, this traditional practice of waiting in the entrance foyer is not expected of foreigners. Still, unless one has already participated in a sesshin conducted by the roshi in Europe or America, thereby demonstrating one's ardor and capacity for zazen, one is not permitted to come to the temple for less than a full year's commitment. Sanzen is not available at all until one proves oneself in residence. These procedures have a rationale. The difficulty of the daily schedule, the unrelenting frequency of sesshins, the intense cold of winter, the heat and humidity and mosquitoes of summer, and the ever-present barriers of language and culture are formidable obstacles. Few foreigners stick it out. Even the Japanese, busy with their own version of material consumerism, shy away.

Philip Kapleau's own experience in Japan naturally colors *The Three Pillars of Zen*. There is a perspective of practice that is characteristically Japanese—especially of the era during which he trained. It is evident, for example, in the following passages:

> Zazen that leads to Self-realization is . . . an intense inner struggle to gain control over the mind and then to use it, like a silent missile, to penetrate the barrier of the five senses and the discursive intellect....
> It demands energy, determination, and courage. Yasutani Roshi calls it "a battle between the opposing forces of delusion and *bodhi* [enlightenment]." This state of mind has been vividly described in these words, said to have been uttered by the Buddha as he sat beneath the Bo tree making his supreme effort, and often quoted in the zendo during sesshin: "Though only my skin, sinews, and bones remain and my blood and flesh dry up and wither away, yet never from this seat will I stir until I have attained full enlightenment."

> One should with clenched teeth, and with tongue pressing on palate, subdue, crush, and overpower the mind.

Zen master Hakuin, who revitalized Zen in late-medieval Japan, followed this approach in his early training. He gritted his teeth, forced his mind into submission through sheer willpower—and became such a nervous wreck that he could no longer function normally. He even quit practice for a time, so high-strung and agitated had he become. Hakuin later wrote that it was not until he had learned from a hermit a way of visualizing a healing elixir that he was able to loosen that tight energy. The hermit's method allowed Hakuin to reconnect with his *tanden*, a center in the lower belly. Only then could he settle down and resume his practice.

For some people, the depiction of the Way as a battle is accurate and compelling. For others, of gentler persuasion, it is a disaster. To Roshi Kapleau's credit, when it became obvious that the method of clenched-teeth force was not universally effective, the style of teaching at the Rochester Zen Center gradually changed. It is evolving there to this day, in the capable hands of Sensei Bodhin Kjolhede, Roshi's successor. Sensei Kjolhede and other second-generation teachers in the West, having experienced traditional training (or a close version of it), are developing new approaches that seem suited to the Western psyche. As a result, a wide variety of teaching styles are now available, a situation far different from the days when the first Zen temples and practice centers were established in the West.

The Buddha said, "Be a lamp unto yourselves." In the end, mustn't we take responsibility for our own practice? We cannot expect a teacher to do it for us, nor can we blindly follow a way of teaching that is counter to our deepest intuitions. Still, having said that, we have to stop a moment. Zen practice is about moving beyond one's habitual ways of experiencing life, so that the true nature of reality is revealed. So long as we continue to operate through habits and assumptions, true experience escapes us. To that end, masters have sometimes relied on extreme measures to push a student beyond his/her usual mind-state. This is the case not just in Zen, but also in other Buddhist sects and spiritual traditions. While one can question the necessity of some of these tough measures, one must be careful before condemning a strict teacher on this basis alone.

When the training is too easy, a common pitfall is to slip into a middling state of practice, with moments of real application and much longer stretches of relative neglect. This is perhaps the greatest danger to Zen in the West: that in our efforts to make Zen palatable to Western students, the intensity of practice that brings genuine results will be lost. As Zen continues to evolve outside Japan, there is increasing risk of throwing the baby out with the bath water, sacrificing the merits of rigorous practice in a rush to reject forms that seem alien.

One such practice not so palatable to modern Americans is seniority. In Japan, seniority is based on two factors: whether or not a person is ordained, and the date of entry into the temple. Monks and nuns, in order of entrance, are above laypeople, who are also ranked in order of entrance. How long you have been practicing in your life is not relevant. And if you leave for some time, when you return you are back at the bottom of the standings until the next person arrives. The word of anyone "above" you is law, and unquestionable. Just do it, whether the directive is reasonable or unreasonable, good or bad. The rule does not say "Anyone more mature is ranked higher," much less "Everyone is ranked equally." Obviously this system creates many challenging situations. At its worst it can lead to hazing, but at its best it is an opportunity to develop openness, resilience, and flexibility—to a degree unparalleled in ordinary life. Perhaps there is a Western way of producing this same result. But many Western Dharma centers that strive to downplay hierarchy thereby lose a rather amazing possibility for spiritual growth.

ZEN WITHOUT AIR-CONDITIONING Recognition of the drawbacks of samurai-style Zen should not be construed as an excuse to avoid effort, discipline, or (at times) harshness. On the contrary, the training at Sogenji taxes one to the utmost. In Japan, the cold of winter and the heat of summer are naturally occurring challenges. Japan has limited energy resources, so heating and cooling are very expensive. In addition, traditional architecture is not air-tight; to heat and cool such porous buildings to Western standards would be inordinately costly. The Japanese have a long tradition of dealing with the cold in winter by judicious use of small areas of radiant heat, such as the *kotatsu*, a sunken pit with a small charcoal fire, or the *rentan*, a large portable pot with a large tube of charcoal burning in it. Both of these methods require fresh air, windows and doors ajar, to avoid the danger of carbon-monoxide poisoning; in any case, they are never expected to heat the amount of area customarily heated in an American home.

More modern heating methods include electric carpets, heated toilet seats, and electric cushions (not in monasteries!). The kotatsu has become a set of electric coils mounted under the top of a low table, with a quilt spreading out from all four sides. One tucks one's legs under the table where the warmth is, covers one's knees with the quilt, and bundles up the rest of the body with a padded house-jacket and extra underwear (wonderful long underwear abounds in Japan). There are also little chemical pouches called *kairo*, activated by removing the outer wrapping and shaking the inner pouch until it begins to make heat. The kairo can then be tucked inside one's clothing—but not against bare skin, as it can produce a burn intense enough to peel skin.

The bone-chilling cold of a damp winter in Japan cannot be fully comprehended unless one has experienced it. Conditions are like winter camping without being able to go inside for months. In the zendo, one is generally not allowed to wear an overcoat or a blanket or a hat (to cover a shaved head). Whatever insulation one adopts against the cold has to be worn under the *koromo* (monk's or nun's robe), the *hakama* (long skirt worn by laymen and laywomen), or the *samugi* (work clothing). Like a little kid out in the snow so bundled up she can't move, I found that I could not add clothing beyond a certain point, because it became impossible to bend my knees enough to sit in zazen. We did sesshins in below-freezing temperatures without any heat at all. Finally, in January, a small kerosene stove was brought into the drafty zendo "to prevent frostbite."

The Japanese bath, which can keep one warm for hours afterward, is sometimes a help, but not always. You must strip down in below-freezing weather before entering the warm water. And if your duties have taken too long, the water will have cooled down by the time it is your turn. Then you have a choice of sitting in tepid water and freezing air, or going without bathing.

In early March, the liquid song of the nightingale is nothing short of wondrous. It means the bird has returned from migration, and spring really might come after all. By the time April rolls around and the weather begins to hint at some actual warmth, one is exhausted from the daily struggle to keep warm through the long cold winter months.

And then it is summer—intensely hot, humid, and full of tenacious mosquitoes that swarm and bite in spite of slathered repellant. We sat in sesshin in 98-percent humidity with the thermometer close to 100 degrees and not a breeze stirring. Rivers of sweat stream down one's body, but tying back or rolling up one's sleeves is not allowed. I was convinced that all mosquito repellants were useless until one unforgettable week in late July when the roshi outlawed mosquito coils because of a small accidental fire involving one of them. With the coils gone, the mosquitoes feasted relentlessly.

Yet something incredible happened at Sogenji. One simply does not have the energy, after dealing with the rigors of practice and climate, to keep up facades or hang onto old personality patterns. The weather intensifies and assists one's practice in a way that is difficult to experience under easier conditions.

One icy winter morning I was doing *takuhatsu*, ritualized almsgathering, which is also a means of going forth to express the Dharma.

During takuhatsu, we stride along chanting *"Hooooooo"* ("Dharma")
until we come to the first doorway unoccupied by a member of our group. We stand before that door with hands palm-to-palm, continuing to chant, until someone comes out and puts a donation into our out-stretched bag. (If it becomes obvious that no one is home or no one is interested, we move on.) Like my companions, I wore a broad straw hat, a robe hiked up to my knees, thin cotton leggings wrapped around my calves, and open sandals on my bare feet. Standing before a doorway in the cold, I unexpectedly found myself in a miniature patch of sunshine. Suddenly, *everything was utterly miraculous!* Not because I was desper-ate, but because cold is miraculous, sun is miraculous, standing there chanting is miraculous—*all life* is miraculous. The experience was so powerful that I was full of joy for a long time afterward. And I could not have understood what I understood without all that went before it, including getting very cold and very hot and very tired and doing quite a lot of zazen.

Another winter day, late in the afternoon, I was walking to the doc-tor's for medicine for frostbite, and I passed some winter plum trees in full bloom. Seeing the delicate blossoms and breathing their exquisite perfume was an experience unlike any I have ever had. It brought new meaning to an old Zen verse:

> But for the chill winds of winter that bite into the bone,
> how can the plum blossom regale me with its piercing fragrance?

Again, I could not have appreciated the true spirit of that verse without those intense winters and summers in the temple in Japan.

We had few choices: be unbearably miserable, leave, or intensify the practice. So the practice went deeper, far deeper than it is likely to go in a nice warm zendo in winter or a comfortably air-conditioned zendo in summer. Such clarity, such joy, such a feeling of lightness and right-ness—and such gratitude for the circumstances that gave rise to these qualities!

At Mountain Gate temple, outside Santa Fe, we had our first sesshin in January of 1998. The adobe zendo has been built entirely with volunteer labor and donated materials. When the beams went up, there was snow on the ground *inside*. The brick-on-sand floor (traditional in New

BISHOP

Mexico) had not yet been laid, so the day before sesshin we leveled the still-damp mud floor as best we could. We screwed all the "button board" to the altar wall, put together sitting platforms of plywood and two-by-fours, and built a temporary altar of two-by-fours topped with an extra piece of button board. There was no running water, and the toilet was in an outhouse.

The windows, luckily, were in. The doors, which had been quickly installed a few days before, swelled in the dampness; by the end of sesshin we faced the prospect of going in and out through the windows. The walls lacked insulation, and the "roof" was two silver tarps nailed to the outside of the adobe walls. The only source of heat was a tiny kerosene stove, which we had to turn off at night because of the danger of the fumes. There was no electricity, so before dawn and after dark we did zazen—and attempted to read our chant books—by kerosene lantern. Temperatures outside hovered slightly above zero degrees. In spite of it all (or because of it?), it turned out to be a very powerful inaugural sesshin.

Can Joshu and Yasutani Roshi and Roshi Kapleau and our other ancestors in Zen continue to inspire us to see deeply into our true nature through American, Polish, or Israeli forms of Zen practice? Some will argue that we can do better practice without having to deal with extreme conditions. I hope this is so, though in my own experience it is not. In our practice in the West, will some other means evolve to address the perils of complacency? Or will we simply take some of the fire out of the practice in the name of comfort? *The Three Pillars of Zen* has spurred countless people to practice and will continue to do so. At least the foundation is there. Where we go now is up to each one of us.

Is American Zen Too Comfortable?

10 | Seeing the Ox: A Second Look

SUNYANA GRAEF

"Here, read this," my professor said, handing me an open book. We were on our way to Rochester, New York, where I was about to attend a seven-day meditation retreat (*sesshin*)—my precipitous introduction to Zen practice. During the several-hour trip, I read story after story of people who had come to enlightenment, people who had been bathed in a "delicious, unspeakable delight," who had disappeared into a "dazzling stream of illumination," who had experienced a "joy like no other." Well, here it was: salvation, a way out of misery. This was just what I had been looking for in every misbegotten place under the sun. My years of confusion and mental turmoil were about to end.

I was wrong. Sesshin was torture, pure and simple. I struggled with my mind; I struggled with my body. With every muscle I pushed and fought my way to *kensho* (initial enlightenment). At the end of the week—nothing. I dissolved into tears, convinced that I was the only one who had not achieved enlightenment. I resolved never to attend another sesshin; clearly I was a Zen failure. Somehow in my rapt yet inattentive reading of the kensho stories in *The Three Pillars of Zen*, I had failed to notice that most of those people had not come to enlightenment at their first sesshin, nor at their second, but only after years of solid training and sesshin experience.

It has been more than thirty years since I first read those stories. Over time, they have become an unsettling question for me. I wonder, Did the enlightenment accounts in *The Three Pillars* point the way, or did they mislead, sometimes woefully so?

Two months after my first sesshin I decided to give it another a try, then another, and another, and so on through the years until I lost count. Although the need for serious training and ongoing practice became indisputable, I still held out for the grail of deeper and deeper enlightenment. My practice became so focused on "breaking through" that I neglected other aspects of training—the cultivation of compassion, for one. Herein lies the double-edged sword of those stories. For some people, they provided the inspiration to begin practicing and the motivation to keep going despite the hardships innate in spiritual work. For others, they led to a warped view of Zen practice.

As students of Roshi Kapleau, every one of us had read *The Three Pillars*. But of all the outstanding material within those covers, it was the kensho stories that held the most intense fascination for many of us twenty-year-olds. Indeed, the greater our confusion and desperation, the greater our obsession with enlightenment. And there were a lot of confused, desperate people coming to the Zen Center in the years just after *The Three Pillars* was published.

For most of us, the lure of kensho was impossible to resist. After all, it seemed to promise exactly the sort of life-altering experience we were searching for:

> Then all at once I was struck as though by lightning, and the next instant heaven and earth crumbled and disappeared. Instantaneously, like surging waves, a tremendous delight welled up in me, a veritable hurricane of delight . . . . This limitless freedom is beyond all expression.
>
> — Mr. K.Y., a Japanese executive

> I feel that through the experience of enlightenment the human mind can expand to the infinity of the cosmos.
>
> — Mr. K.T., a Japanese gardener

Seeing the Ox: A Second Look

This was heady stuff, and we were enthralled by it. In fact, we were so focused on this one goal that we actually kept track. "She finally had kensho!" we would hear whispered excitedly after a sesshin, and we would slip over to give our Dharma sister a meaningful hug. "It was *such* a strong sesshin—*five* people broke through!" we would gloat. Moreover, we believed that people who were enlightened were special, certainly more advanced spiritually, and generally on a somewhat higher plane than those who had not yet seen into their koan. Never mind if the newly awakened Dharma brother became inflated with pride; never mind if his ego still asserted itself in outrageous ways. He was enlightened, and that was what really counted.

The promise of kensho was a driving force of amazing power. Convinced as we were that enlightenment was the sole way to attain peace of mind, we committed ourselves to practice with a fierce, single-minded intensity. We had read the accounts and were certain that our lives would undergo cosmic transformations: we would emerge whole and complete, healed in body and mind.

The turbulent sixties and seventies brought seekers to the Rochester Zen Center in droves. Sesshins, at that time held every month, were always oversubscribed; often more than one hundred applicants vied for the sixty or so seats available in the *zendo* (meditation hall). People had to be turned away, which meant that a system or principle was needed to decide who would contribute most to the sesshin and who would benefit most from it. This unavoidable selection process led to the conclusion that those who attended sittings regularly were more serious about their practice than those who were less regular (or more involved with work or family). Single people with temporary, part-time jobs therefore had a competitive edge when it came to sesshin acceptance.

In those days, sesshins at the Rochester Zen Center had a reputation for being the "boot camp" of Zen training. Roshi Kapleau's *teishos* (Dharma talks) and the monitors' enouragement talks were geared toward helping people summon the determination and energy to break through their koans, justly described as "difficult to penetrate, difficult to unravel, difficult to enter." It was not unusual for students to sit through an entire seven-day sesshin with only a few hours of sleep. Participants would routinely skip meals to dedicate themselves to zazen, sometimes going without eating for several days. The *kyosaku* (encouragement stick) was used incessantly—some would say mercilessly—to rouse sitters to a fevered pitch. On the last few nights of sesshin, those working on the koan Mu were encouraged to bellow *MU!* during the final round of zazen. Then, at the next bell, everyone would jump up to do a type of running meditation, which generated even more energy.

There was fierce competition for the opportunity to attend *dokusan*, the private encounter with the master, since Roshi could see only about half the participants during each of the three two-hour blocks. In the moments before dokusan began, the inspiring words of the monitors, followed by the vigorous whacking of the stick, created an intensity bordering on hysteria. The zendo filled with crackling energy, adrenaline surging, hearts pounding, as everyone waited for Roshi's handbell to signal the start of dokusan. The instant the bell rang, students flew off their mats to be first in the waiting line. Races to dokusan resulted in more than a few injuries over the years. Once Bodhin Kjolhede and I, responding to the bell, jumped off our mats at precisely the same instant. As we hurtled through the zendo doors, we collided, falling to the ground in a heap. The people coming from behind did not even slow down; they just ran around us like a stream flowing past a rock. As for us, we helped each other up, dusted ourselves off, and resumed the race.

The highly charged atmosphere of sesshin was often compared to a pressure cooker, an apt analogy. The pressure was so great that people occasionally broke under the strain. The sound of the kyosaku alone, even without feeling its stinging bite, was enough to dissuade some sitters from attending a second sesshin. All this was done for the purpose of helping students come to awakening. And it worked. It was a rare sesshin conducted by Roshi Kapleau when no one "broke through."

Yet, was the frenzy really necessary? Would people have awakened anyway, without that degree of pressure? Did the kensho stories, which ignited this near-mania, invite discouragement as often as inspiration? There were those who gave way to feelings of envy, even jealousy, towards others who "had..." while they "had not." Some were swamped by feelings of inferiority when, after years attempting to see into the realm of the absolute, they remained firmly planted in duality. Others found themselves constantly waiting for their experiences or mind-states to match those of the people in *The Three Pillars*, especially when they felt that they might be approaching the moment of enlightenment.

Seeing the Ox: A Second Look

KENSHO ACCOUNTS IN PERSPECTIVE The fact is that
Buddhism is a religion of enlightenment. The teachings of Shakyamuni
Buddha, which proclaim that all sentient beings have the potential to
realize their true nature, spring from his profound awakening. We can
say that enlightenment accounts are a kind of *upaya*, or skillful means,
to encourage practitioners to do the work necessary to come to realization. Like the parable of the burning house in the *Lotus Sutra*, in which
people must be induced to flee a fire, we are emboldened to leave our
state of suffering by the promise of treasures yet to come. Even if the
treasure turns out to be gold dust rather than gold nuggets, still it is
something, and we have confirmation that we are traveling in the right
direction. Without the first-hand accounts to point the way, "Zen practice" might well have become nothing more than a New Agey search for
tranquility or states of bliss. Koans are not mantras, and these stories—
and Roshi Kapleau's teaching—never let you forget that.

There is nothing heterodox about divulging kensho experiences. The
descriptions follow a 2,500-year-old tradition of recounting through nar-
rative, song, and verse the circumstances leading to one's awakening.
Take, for example, the *Therigatha*, which contains enlightenment
accounts by nuns during the formative years of Buddhism. In
Nanduttara's story we read, "Seeing the body as it really is, desires have
been rooted out. Coming to birth is ended, and my cravings as well.
Untied from all that binds, my heart is at peace." Sundari-Nanda sings,
"I am careful, quenched, calm, and free," while Patacara says simply,
"When the lamp went out, my mind was freed."[1] Through the long, rich
history of Buddhism and Zen, the enlightenment accounts of countless
masters have been published, often as a means of encouraging and
motivating students. *The Transmission of Light*, a Zen text by Keizan,
contains the enlightenment accounts of fifty-three ancestors, from
Shakyamuni Buddha through the medieval Japanese master Ejo.

There were few, if any, such accounts available to Westerners at the
time *The Three Pillars of Zen* was published. Furthermore, it was somewhat of a revelation to learn that Westerners—both men *and* women—
also had buddha nature and could awaken to it. In the stories we recognize ourselves and sense that we are not alone in our spiritual gropings.
As Zen master Dogen said, "The buddhas and ancestors in the past were
like us, and we will in the future become buddhas and ancestors." If
even one desperate person could find a way out of her misery and come
to awakening, then surely there is hope for us.

GRAEF

Reading the accounts in *The Three Pillars*, one could easily get the impression that kensho is a once-and-for-all, life-altering experience:

> A lifetime has been compressed into one week. A thousand new sensations are bombarding my senses, a thousand new paths are opening before me.
>
> — Mrs. A. M., an American schoolteacher

> The world no longer rides heavily on my back. It is under my belt. I turned a somersault and swallowed it. I am no longer restless. At last I have what I want.
>
> — Mrs. L. T. S., an American artist

> Everything flows smoothly, freely. Everything goes naturally. This limitless freedom is beyond all expression. What a wonderful world!
>
> — Mr. K. Y., a Japanese executive

Some people believed that with kensho they would spontaneously develop new skills: become able to paint, sing, dance, write, act, read minds, remember past lifetimes, perhaps even levitate! So overblown were their expectations that the experience could not help but lack the transformative power they thought it would have. No wonder Roshi Kapleau repeatedly warned, "Don't poison the real with the ideal." Kensho can certainly cause abrupt transformations, but it is never the end of the spiritual road.

In addition, many Zen students assumed that with kensho they would have the same emotional reactions as the writers in *The Three Pillars*. They looked forward to being "struck by a bolt of lightning." Yet a valid kensho can come with little emotional upheaval. According to tradition, Zen master Dogen simply declared, "My eyes are horizontal; my nose is vertical." While there were definitely those who responded with shouts of joy and tears of gratitude, others were chagrined to find that they did not experience any drama at all. Oddly, without the expected fireworks and inversions of heaven and earth, some practitioners actually felt cheated when they finally saw what had always been before their eyes.

From Roshi Kapleau's perspective, awakening, by itself, was never the goal. Ongoing practice, ever-deepening realization, maturity, harmony, compassionate action, and, above all, actualization were his true standards. Kensho was vital, certainly, but it was only an initial step in the long road of spiritual training. Often Roshi would say, "Enlightenment shows you up!" Even after a kensho experience, it is still necessary to

Seeing the Ox: A Second Look

overcome the persistent illusion of ego-I, clean up bad habits, and let go of clinging attachments. And the fruits of practice must be put into action in our everyday lives. *The Three Pillars* points this out in any number of ways. For example, in his introduction to the enlightenment experiences, Kapleau says:

> Zen training stresses the need to ripen an initial awakening through subsequent koan practice and/or *shikantaza* [just sitting] until it thoroughly animates one's life. In other words, to function on the higher level of consciousness brought about by kensho, one must further train oneself to act in accordance with this perception of Truth.

The Ten Oxherding Pictures clearly illustrate the need for consistent dedication to practice after awakening. Although the kensho stories spotlight the third picture in particular—the stage of seeing the Ox—the fourth through tenth pictures map the higher stages of spiritual development to be realized through continued practice. In *The Three Pillars* account of Mr. K. T., Taji Roshi uses the Oxherding Pictures to instruct K. T. after his initial awakening:

> There is a tremendous difference between shallow and deep realization, and these different levels are depicted in the Ten Oxherding Pictures. The depth of your enlightenment is no greater than that shown in the third picture, namely, that of seeing the Ox. . . . Your kensho is such that you can easily lose sight of it if you become lazy and forego further practice. . . . But if you continue with zazen, you will reach the point of grasping the Ox. . . .
>
> Beyond the stage of grasping the Ox is the stage of taming it, followed by riding it, which is a state of awareness in which enlightenment and ego are seen as one and the same. Next, the seventh stage, is that of forgetting the Ox; the eighth, that of forgetting the Ox as well as oneself; the ninth, the grade of grand enlightenment, which penetrates to the very bottom and where one no longer differentiates enlightenment from non-enlightenment.
>
> The last . . . having completely finished one's practice, one moves, as himself, among ordinary people, helping them wherever possible, free from all attachment to enlightenment. To live in this last stage is the aim of life, and its accomplishment may require many cycles of existence.

The section containing Yasutani Roshi's private encounters with

Westerners likewise makes it clear that kensho is only the beginning of the journey. When a student pointed out that certain people become more grasping and egotistical *after* an enlightenment experience, Yasutani Roshi responded:

> With a first enlightenment, the realization of oneness is usually shallow. Yet if one has genuinely perceived, even though dimly, and *continues to practice devotedly for five or ten more years* [emphasis added], his inner vision will expand in depth and magnitude as his character acquires flexibility and purity. One whose actions are still dominated by ego cannot be said to have had a valid enlightenment. Furthermore, an authentic experience not only reveals one's imperfections, but it simultaneously creates the determination to remove them.

In his introduction to Zen master Bassui's Dharma talk and letters, Roshi Kapleau relates that even after coming to awakening, Bassui continued to practice assiduously, until he completely dispelled his persistent question, "Who is the master?"

The moving Iwasaki letters, both the letters themselves and Harada Roshi's comments, treat enlightenment as a by-product of resolute, devoted zazen, not an end in itself. Stated differently, enlightenment is a process without an endpoint:

> YAEKO IWASAKI: Truly I see that there are degrees of depth in enlightenment. . . . I am ashamed [of my defects], and will make every effort to discipline my character. . . . Far from neglecting zazen, I have every intention of strengthening even further my powers of concentration. I am profoundly aware of the need for diligent self-cultivation. . . . I can now appreciate how dangerously one-sided a weak kensho can be.

> HARADA ROSHI: A one-sided realization remains a one-sided realization regardless of how many koans one has passed. What . . . people fail to realize is that their enlightenment is capable of endless enlargement.

Nevertheless, the small mind is amazingly adept at hearing what it wants to hear. Actually, it often does not hear even what it hears, or what it itself is saying. This is one reason why in Buddhism we often say things three times: the first to say it, the second to listen, and the third to have it go to the heart. The danger of distortion is a phenomenon that almost

Seeing the Ox: A Second Look

every teacher faces. In my own case, sensitivity to listeners' perverse ability to misapprehend—to not *just hear*—has made me wary of allowing
my Dharma talks to be recorded. Perhaps if the words are spoken and
then allowed to fade away, ashes to ashes, dust to dust, there will be less
likelihood that they will cause confusion or worse.

But keeping Dharma talks out of circulation does not resolve the
koan of talking about kensho. Simply put, if enlightenment is never
talked about, how will people know it is possible? And if it *is* talked
about, how can that be done in such a way that people will not
become greedy for the experience and overly attached to it as a goal?
I wrestled with this dilemma when I first began teaching. If enlightenment were never talked about, it would be doing violence to the
teaching handed down to me by my teacher. But if it were, I needed
to do so in a way that reflected my own feelings about practice, based
on my training with Roshi Kapleau and my experience at the
Rochester Zen Center.

KENSHO JUST SHOWS THE WAY It is only natural that
there are differences in Roshi Kapleau's teaching style and that of his
successors. The way a teacher expresses the Dharma is a spontaneous
outflowing of his or her understanding, personality, and background.
None of Roshi's successors are his clones. He always made it clear that
a teacher must be free to teach in the way that is most suitable for that
person. He felt this in his marrow. When his Dharma heirs went out on
their own, he offered support and encouragement but never gave unso-
licited advice. I am certain that at times he had to bite his tongue to
keep from doing so, but since I began teaching he has never told me
how to run the Vermont Zen Center or what I was doing wrong.

As a result, I felt free to experiment with aspects of the training. For
example, I was never comfortable with what I saw as the extreme,
samurai-like use of the kyosaku. It seemed to go against the very heart of
practice—namely, that you are training because you want to liberate all
sentient beings. To me, it felt contradictory to strike people with a stick to
encourage them to do what they were already doing, had vowed to do,
wanted to do, and were striving mightily to do. Moreover, if you had to
be hit in order to do the work, wouldn't you become dependent upon
someone pushing and exhorting you to do what should be your own
responsibility? If you use a crutch when there is no injury, your leg muscles will atrophy. In the end, you will not be able to walk without it. I

hoped that if the stick were used much less, people would learn to rely more on themselves to rouse energy and strengthen determination.

Still, it was not an easy decision to let go of the kyosaku. Part of me actually wondered whether the spirit of Rinzai or Manjushri would chop off my head for such heresy. In fairness, it must be said that there are those for whom the stick is a tremendous aid, helping to banish sleepiness during long hours of zazen, giving a jolt of energy when the body-mind is flagging, and clearing the mind of distracting thoughts. What to do? Eventually, a solution appeared: simply give people a choice. If someone wants the stick, it is offered. If not, that's fine. Every now and then we have a Rohatsu sesshin where the stick is not used at all. (Traditionally, Rohatsu is when the stick is used most heavily, making it a particularly severe sesshin.) Do people still work hard without the constant encouragement and pressure of the kyosaku? You bet they do. The unique conditions and structure of a sesshin—the hours of zazen, the silence, dokusan, chanting, and talks—exert an inward push that is impossible to avoid.

As a corollary to this low-key use of the kyosaku, I try to de-emphasize kensho and place greater emphasis on the necessity to *practice for the sake of practice*. Not that I don't talk about awakening—I do. It comes up in Dharma talks frequently. But in sesshin I try to not to make even the slightest suggestion that if you do not come to awakening in this sesshin, your practice is deficient, or you are not working hard enough, or your aspiration is half-hearted. I hope this will help people avoid being ensnared by the trap of kensho obsession. In particular, I hope that Zen students will not fall into the mistaken belief that one who has had kensho is automatically wiser, greater in stature, and more knowledgeable about everything than those who have not yet awakened.

No matter how hard a teacher tries, there will always be practitioners who are preoccupied with kensho. Sometimes this takes absurd forms. Once a young man attending a workshop told me, "I've had eight kenshos!" After questioning him, I concluded that he had had eight *makyos* (illusory visions). At a sesshin a first-time participant waltzed right out of the Zen Center during a round of zazen and went on a little celebratory jaunt, claiming, "I've just had kensho and I don't need to bother with sitting anymore." Although she could not answer even one testing question, she still insisted that she was enlightened: "I've read the accounts, and my experience is the same." Nothing would convince her otherwise.

Seeing the Ox: A Second Look

Clearly there is a danger of confusing kensho with bizarre or altered states of consciousness. Therefore, as *The Three Pillars of Zen* reveals, it is essential that a teacher confirm the experience. Without the scrutiny of a qualified teacher, without submitting to the "black piercing eyes of a devil," there is virtually no way to know whether or not one has had a bona fide experience of awakening.

Another danger arises when enlightenment is separated from compassion. If enlightened wisdom is not expressed through compassionate action, it is not true enlightenment. Without compassion, practice becomes stale and egocentric. "Even if some benefit accrues," writes one master, "because confined to oneself alone, it cannot but be small."[2] Likewise, compassionate action must be grounded in enlightened wisdom. Pursuing one at the expense of the other stunts spiritual growth. Unfortunately, when practitioners are striving to realize wisdom, compassion is all too often looked upon as the poor relation.

Strangely, while we accept that we must exert ourselves to realize wisdom, we mistakenly believe that compassion will spring forth full-bodied at the moment of awakening. But this is not so. Compassion is latent within us, but it must be expressed to be made real, and it must be developed to reach its full potential. The *Avatamsaka Sutra* says:

> All the buddhas and *tathagatas* [enlightened ones] regard the heart of great compassion as the essence. Great compassion arises towards sentient beings; depending on this great compassion, the heart of enlightenment arises; and depending on the enlightened heart, true insight becomes perfected.

Compassion, then, is fundamental. Through it, the dynamic outflowing of our awakened Mind becomes the bodhisattva Avalokiteshvara's one thousand hands and eyes.

Taoist sages teach that courage arises from compassion. Doing this work is not easy at first, but with great compassion in the heart it is possible. No longer does one practice in order to become enlightened; one practices for the sake of all beings who suffer. Zen master Torei states it concisely:

> By the power of the vow of great compassion, all karmic obstacles disappear, and all merit and virtue/strength are completed. No principle remains obscure; all ways are walked by it; no wisdom remains unattained, no virtue incomplete.[3]

Those who realize that wisdom must be integrated into their lives through compassionate action are motivated to keep working despite all obstacles. Those whose motivation to practice is solely to succor themselves will find a thousand reasons to avoid persevering when difficulties arise.

Still, the lure of kensho is hard to ignore. Compassion, we believe, is what you learn in Girl Scouts, nothing very glamorous. Enlightenment, on the other hand, seems really special, the mystical wisdom you get from a master. It is something we want *for ourselves*, to make us spiritual human beings full of love and light and joy. At the beginning of training, it is a rare Zen student who, when asked about his or her aspiration, will not say, "I need to change my life. I want to become enlightened." What this often means is, "I am unhappy and need to find a way to make my life better right now." The emphasis is on the "I," closely followed by the "right now." The unspoken assumption is that kensho will do the trick, and from then on it will be smooth sailing.

For whatever reasons, the enlightenment stories in *The Three Pillars* do gloss over the inescapable vicissitudes of Zen practice. As the Japanese put it, "Seven times down, eight times up—such is life." The accounts say very little about the setbacks and plateaus in sitting, or the riptide pull of habit patterns, or the disheartening reversions to ego-centered modes of behavior. Also omitted are the ongoing battles with concentration: so long as we have a body, we will have thoughts. Then there are the periods of self-doubt and internal conflict, when one asks oneself, "Did I *really* have an awakening? Is *this* all there is? Why isn't my life transformed?" In our darkest moments, we even suffer a loss of faith: "Did my teacher pass me too easily? Does she really know what she's doing? Maybe her teacher passed *her* too easily!" The stories do not address the truth that ripening karma, in all its multifarious manifestations, remains operative. In terms of the Ten Oxherding Pictures, when the kensho accounts spotlight only the third Oxherding picture, the modulating effects of the preceding and following pictures are minimized or lost altogether.

Kensho—the merest glimpse into the realm of the absolute—just shows the way, nothing more. It does not produce an actual transformation. That is done through continuous daily practice, observance of the precepts, and compassionate action. Many people believe that with enlightenment the hard work is done, and now they can relax and enjoy themselves. Actually, the hard work has just begun. In time, their lives

Seeing the Ox: A Second Look

will indeed be transformed. But it does not happen with an initial ken-sho; it does not happen all at once; and it does not happen without con-siderable effort.

The truth is, with a shallow one-sided kensho (almost universally, ini-tial kenshos are shallow), you cannot truly be called enlightened. You have merely exchanged seeing with only one eye for seeing with only the other. In the first case, you are half-blinded by the aspect of dis-crimination, taken in by the usual distinctions among phenomena. In the second, you are half-blinded by the aspect of emptiness, able to intuit oneness but unable to actualize it. If you are not adequately pre-pared for the experience of awakening, are too careless or immature to sustain continued practice, or become attached to the experience itself, the benefits of the awakening will be extremely limited.

Nevertheless, it would be a sad mistake to conclude that kensho is val-ueless. As a sutra says, "If you are bound yourself, you cannot untie another's bonds." Kensho loosens the knots so that we can untangle our-selves and eventually help others do the same. With continued training, deeper awakenings will follow. There are few indeed—Yaeko Iwasaki being one of them—who have come to deep enlightenment in one fell swoop, and even Yaeko began with kensho. Kensho shows the way, set-ting our feet on the road to full enlightenment.

In the Iwasaki letters, Harada Roshi points out, "It is only with full enlightenment that it is possible to put your Zen into practice in daily life." This can be interpreted to mean that only after profound enlight-enment does one's daily life naturally come into accord with one's realization. That is, there is no compulsion, no self-conscious effort to incorporate what one has realized into one's everyday activities. It sim-ply is one's life. Only with this degree of understanding is the illusion of ego obliterated. There is no self, no other. What one sees, hears, and does, one is. Things are as they are without distortion. Daily life is the expression of practice; practice is the expression of compassion. One sits not just for oneself, but for the sake of all sentient beings. Thus, no mat-ter what, one will continue on and on. Zen master Hakuin's words ring clear: "Exert yourselves, students, for the Buddha Way is deep and far. Let everyone know that the farther you enter the sea the deeper it becomes, and the higher you climb a mountain the taller it gets."

Have I resolved the koan of *The Three Pillars* kensho accounts? I don't know. Like all koans, it is a bottomless fount. Ten years from now, things may look very different to me. But there is something I am certain will never change: my profound gratitude to Philip Kapleau for writing *The Three Pillars of Zen*, and my even deeper gratitude to him for being my teacher. And yes, Roshi, thank you for those "difficult to penetrate, difficult to unravel, difficult to enter" wonderful enlightenment stories.

Seeing the Ox: A Second Look

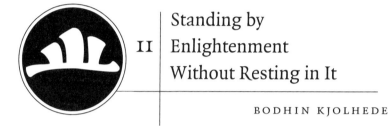

Standing by
11 | Enlightenment
Without Resting in It

BODHIN KJOLHEDE

W hen I first opened *The Three Pillars of Zen*, in March of
1970, I only managed to get halfway through the first chap-
ter before setting it aside, bored. It was altogether too
grounded in practice. Where were the rarefied heights of metaphysical
abstraction that had been so transporting in the writings of D. T. Suzuki
and Alan Watts? Those books had left me feeling bathed in higher consciousness, but this one was exhorting me to *work*.

It took a personal crisis, a few months later, to pierce the clouds of
philosophical reverie that continued to beguile me. While hitchhiking
home through Canada to Michigan, I was strip-searched by U.S. cus-
toms agents at the Detroit-Windsor Tunnel. They found the small stash
of peyote buttons I was carrying, and threw me into a crowded holding
cell on the ninth floor of the Detroit city jail. It was a night in hell. I
emerged physically unharmed but shaken by the wretched state to
which I had fallen — especially in the eyes of my heretofore adoring parents. My sense of myself and the world had suddenly come loose from
its moorings.

My angst now at critical mass, I returned to the book and found my way to the enlightenment accounts. As I read the individual narratives, the Third Noble Truth—*there is a way out of suffering*—flashed across the dark sky of my nonreligious mind like exploding fireworks. Seeing this staggering new vista was the Big Bang of my spiritual life. Galvanized, I went back and waded into Yasutani Roshi's introductory lectures. Now they had become absorbing, and led me effortlessly into the master-student encounters (*dokusan*). These offered practical instruction, suddenly welcome, demystifying the teaching even as they testified to its timelessness. And the Dharma talk by Zen master Bassui was like no talk I had ever heard, ringing out with the authority of realization.

Above all, it was the enlightenment accounts that elevated my heartbeat. In the books of Watts and Suzuki I had heard of awakening, but here were blow-by-blow descriptions told first-hand by people who had been there. Those descriptions mirrored some elements of my own transcendent experiences with psychedelic drugs. Mescaline had revealed a world of cosmic love, ordinarily obscured by false appearances, in which every individual was a breathtakingly unique expression of ultimate worth. These hallucinogenic experiences had been transitory, but now with the promise of enlightenment, I thought, they could be recovered and secured. I was on my way home!

That was in 1970, and since then I have reread *The Three Pillars* (sections of it anyway) numerous times. Most recently I read it aloud in a recording studio, to produce an audiobook. Once again the text came alive for me, especially the enlightenment section. This was something of a surprise, for having had some similar experiences of my own over the years, I half-expected that such stories would now have lost some of their impact. But their power held, fresh and undiminished.

THE VALIDITY OF AWAKENING   In recent years, statements have appeared in articles and books, sometimes by Zen teachers, suggesting that the Zen presented in *The Three Pillars* is misleading in its emphasis on *kensho* (initial awakening). This critique may be quite valid or profoundly flawed, depending on the understanding of the person making it. The danger of published enlightenment accounts is twofold: first, they can provoke in the reader a grasping state of mind, the very antithesis of our essential mind; and second, they can give the impression that an initial awakening is the arrival point of Zen practice.

Standing by Enlightenment Without Resting in It

There is no doubt that a dramatically written enlightenment account has the potential to stimulate desire. What, after all, could be more enticing than a vivid description of satori, the winning draw in the grand lottery of spirituality? It is no wonder that Publishers' Clearinghouse devotes such fanfare to filming grand-prize winners opening their front doors to receive the good news. In Zen, we too would like everyone to enter the sweepstakes. "You can't win unless you enter!" In spiritual practice, unlike a lottery, everyone wins just by playing—if one is sincere and keeps at it long enough.

Roshi Kapleau has admitted that when he went back to Japan to enter Zen training, all he wanted was to "grab kensho and run." This acquisitive attitude to practice may have obstructed his progress as much as it fueled his efforts. But it seems to have kept him interested long enough so that by the time he got what he sought, his aspiration had been purified and broadened. The momentum his practice had gathered while he was grasping for the gold ring carried him beyond his spiritual materialism.

Egoistic desire, or greed, is understood in Buddhism as one of the "three poisons" that give rise to human suffering. If enlightenment stories merely incited greed, it would be best to keep them secret or even destroy them. Yet human beings also have exalted desires that can be nourished by descriptions of awakening. In Pali, the original language of Buddhism, a distinction is drawn between higher and lower desires. *Tanha* denotes the latter, and really means craving, the egoistic desire to *have* something. *Chanda*, on the other hand, signifies the desire to *do* something. The highest aspiration in Mahayana Buddhism is to attain enlightenment for the sake of all sentient beings. This intention is voiced in Zen centers and temples throughout the world in the four bodhisattva vows:

> All beings, without number, I vow to liberate.
> Endless blind passions I vow to uproot.
> Dharma gates, beyond measure, I vow to penetrate.
> The Great Way of Buddha I vow to attain.

Rarely, if ever, do we find a beginner whose response to the lure of enlightenment is motivated purely by altruism. Usually it is the opposite: although people come to practice sick of their selfish desires, those egoistic drives still predominate for some time. Eventually, lower desires can be transmuted into higher ones.

KJOLHEDE

Zen has a robust history of monks waging all-out assaults on the forces of delusion, stopping at nothing to achieve liberation. The Japanese monk Bassui, whose Dharma talk and letters are included in *The Three Pillars*, would climb a tree and do *zazen* (meditation) on a branch, night after night, oblivious to wind, rain, and cold. Hakuin became so absorbed in his practice that he would go day and night without sleep, forgetting even to eat. Bankei endured fourteen years of hardship, sitting alone in the mountains and other remote places, before his enlightenment. The Chinese monk Shih-shuang reportedly kept a gimlet by his side as he meditated: "whenever he felt drowsy, he stuck it into his thigh."[1]

What drove these spiritual titans to such extremes of exertion? At base it is always a thirst for truth, but less exalted pressures also come into play, both from within and without. The records tell us that for Hakuin, among others, it was fear of hell and rebirth. Among Asians especially, shame (at the prospect of losing face or causing others to lose face) has sometimes been the impetus. Because additives are mixed in with basic bodhisattvic aspirations, an absolutely pure motivation would be as unreal as an absolutely pure person.

We practice in accordance with our karmic tendencies. Each of us brings to the path our emotional afflictions and other habit-energies, like bringing excess baggage on a trip. Indeed, if we did not have these propensities we would not need to practice. So we work with what we have, our practice driven by our cravings and aversions as well as the longing to transcend those impurities. It is all the functioning of Mind. Roshi Kapleau used to note, "From the point of view of our true nature, there is only true nature. From the point of view of ego, there is only ego."

In our desperate striving for liberation, we may resort to painful, even brutal measures. In one sense, those efforts are misguided to the extent that they arise from a grasping mind-state. Indeed, when practice becomes inordinately zealous, is it by nature dualistic? Yes, even the desire for awakening—awakening to the essentially nondual nature of reality—is dualistic. But in the beginning of any endeavor one must bring forth an intention. Without will, nothing can be accomplished. Later that effort becomes purified, until one can surrender to a force that transcends the self's desires.

My experience in working with Zen students has revealed that men, more than women, are disposed to see kensho as an external goal to be won. The material in *The Three Pillars of Zen* supports this observation: the accounts that describe the pursuit of kensho in the most acquisitive and martial terms are by the men. We also find a partial explanation in *The Three Pillars*: Yasutani Roshi suggests that men are more prone than women to play with ideas—and what idea is more alluring than kensho? On the other hand, the women's stories are characterized by a style of searching and wondering. The latter approach may be more mature and effective, but one must grow into it.

Zen students who are preoccupied with kensho as a goal can nonetheless marshal that passion in the service of the Dharma. In its early years the Rochester Zen Center had a reputation as the "boot camp" of American Zen. Most of its members were in their twenties, with energy to burn. The strenuous use of the *kyosaku* (encouragement stick), the explosive rushes to dokusan, and other gung-ho features of training suited many of us just fine. Young bucks, like anyone else, will engage with the practice as they need to. This may mean huffing and puffing in pursuit of enlightenment (there are worse outlets for testosterone) until the alchemical powers of zazen transmute grasping into questioning and other modes of introspection.

Those who wish to abide in doctrinal purity (that too is a goal) may deny any desire to attain liberation. Indeed, this position is common enough that the Japanese have a name for it: *buji* Zen. According to buji Zen, to speak of becoming enlightened is a contradiction in terms since we are all intrinsically enlightened. In *The Three Pillars*, Yasutani Roshi warns against this approach as an "egregious error" that negates the validity of awakening.

One of the remarkable aspects of *The Three Pillars of Zen* is how far it goes in presenting the opposite of buji Zen. Probably no other English-language book on Buddhism is so unabashedly focused on attainment. Yasutani Roshi, stating flatly that "Buddhism is a religion of enlightenment," cites the aim of satori as the fourth and highest level of aspiration. He exhorts his students toward kensho with the steadiness of a drumbeat, and the kensho accounts themselves are testimonials to the power of spiritual ambition.

Some of the accounts are reminiscent of war exploits, Olympic sports contests, or assaults on Himalayan peaks. This quality of mythic struggle is what many of us found so compelling about *The Three Pillars*. Yet now I find myself wincing at some of Yasutani Roshi's motivational remarks and the goal-driven language used by contributors in describing their pursuit of awakening. "Getting" satori or kensho is an oft-used expression, alternating with "attaining," "reaching," "achieving," "accomplish-

KJOLHEDE

ing," and so on. Such language is dualistic, and nakedly so. But I don't remember wincing at all when I first read it.

The publication of awakening accounts is nothing new. Every Buddhist country has its corpus of such stories, dating back to well-known depictions of Shakyamuni's life. Other religious traditions have equivalent genres. The collection in *The Three Pillars* is unprecedented in that the eleven contemporary women and men all came to awakening as laypersons. Spiritually sensitive people who relate awakening experiences (their own or others') are usually aware that such accounts may stimulate longing in the reader, but they believe that the inspirational value outweighs the potential compounding of desire.

The true inspirational power of a kensho account kicks in when, instead of provoking wistfulness and envy, it directs one back to one's own practice. I weathered physical pain, disappointment, frustration, and self-doubt for years, before a particularly stirring kensho account galvanized me to reach the next level of effort. The author of the account, which was published in the Rochester Zen Center's quarterly periodical, was an uncle figure of whom I was very fond. We had sat next to each other through many meditation retreats (*sesshin*), but I had thought, in my ignorance, that he was too intellectual to come to awakening. His vivid description of his own travails and sudden turnabout had an electrifying impact on me, evoking tears of joy. Gone was the ache at reading of another's "success." Instead, a profound new conviction arose: if he could do it, so can I! My faith now unwavering, at the next sesshin I finally passed the koan Mu.

The Three Pillars of Zen appeals not only to the heavy breathers among readers but to all who long for liberation. To be human is to have this longing, though relatively few of us are conscious of it. Those who are not will probably not respond to *The Three Pillars* any more than they would to the vigorous teaching style of Hakuin, Bassui, and other fierce Zen masters who championed the experience of enlightenment. Inasmuch as *The Three Pillars* presents the teachings of Yasutani Roshi, its perspective is that of the Sanbokyodan school (lit., Three Treasures Association), which Yasutani founded. In an article on this lineage that appeared in the *Japanese Journal of Religious Studies*, scholar Robert Sharf asserts that its most distinctive feature is "the unrelenting emphasis on kensho and the vigorous tactics used to bring it about."[2]

Standing by Enlightenment Without Resting in It

Enlightenment is an experience in time, but it is also beyond the realm of time. The timeless dimension of enlightenment lies at the very heart of Zen understanding. Essentially, the relationship between practice and enlightenment is an acausal one: zazen is not just a means to an end but is itself the functioning of our enlightened nature. This nonattainable aspect of enlightenment has a decidedly minor key in *The Three Pillars*, and those who resonate to it more than to the promise of kensho may find greater inspiration from another modern Zen classic, *Zen Mind, Beginner's Mind*, by Shunryu Suzuki Roshi. Written in a simple and informal style, *Zen Mind, Beginner's Mind* presents the more patient, quietistic approach of traditional Soto Zen. As such, it serves as a complement to *The Three Pillars*. I have much respect for the teachings of Suzuki Roshi, but his book has never moved me. Our responses to different teaching styles are a matter of affinity. Those of us who feel compelled to confirm our buddha nature through realization will be drawn to a teacher who exhorts us to dedicate ourselves to that goal. Those who feel no such urgency may instead find *The Three Pillars* raw and strained in its focus on kensho.

Whatever our temperament, we risk losing the very marrow of our faith when we deny the possibility of awakening. Yet the virus of buji Zen has already begun to infect our tradition here in the West. There are Dharma centers where to refer to enlightenment even indirectly is taboo. Sometimes this is a valid constraint, as in the case of students engaged in casual conversations; the "Great Matter" should not be reduced to the level of bingo-hall chatter. But a teacher who never mentions the possibility of awakening, the most profoundly transforming experience a human being can have, does his or her students a disservice. A teacher may justify such an omission on doctrinal grounds: "Fundamentally, we are all buddhas, and 'enlightenment' and 'ignorance' are just relative constructs of the mind." Indeed, one could cite many great masters who spoke in the same way. Yet those masters had earned the right, through their deep realization, to make that kind of statement. Unfortunately, too many Zen teachers today who refuse to acknowledge the importance of awakening do so because they have not yet confirmed it through their own experience. In fact, they wouldn't know their true nature if they found it in their soup.

Neither beginners nor veteran practitioners of Zen need apologize, then, for having a burning desire to realize their true nature. There can be no higher purpose to human life. In Mahayana Buddhism

KJOLHEDE

(which includes Zen), the aspiration to awaken is itself regarded as wondrously rare. Like fish in water seeking air, those with the will to enlightenment sense and aspire to a reality for which the evidence, initially at least, is scant. So it is something of a miracle that, clouded as we are by ignorance, we become aware of enlightenment even as a possibility.

KENSHO IS NOT A ZEN VERSION OF HEAVEN Besides the view that *The Three Pillars of Zen* manifests something of a fixation on "getting" kensho, a related critique of the book is that it gives the impression that kensho represents the culmination of Zen practice. This criticism does have some validity, especially if the meaning of kensho is not clear.

The Three Pillars often uses the words "kensho" and "satori" in keeping with its predominantly Japanese flavor (it was written by Kapleau in Japan, and originally published there). Its glossary tells us that "semantically, kensho and satori have virtually the same meaning and are often used interchangeably," but that "the term satori implies a deeper experience." Generally kensho refers to a first, incomplete awakening experience, what is sometimes called "entering the first gate." In other words, it is hardly the ultimate spiritual experience. *The Three Pillars* reminds us of this repeatedly and explicitly. In his introductory lectures, Yasutani Roshi makes the following statements:

Usually a first kensho is shallow.

At the beginning, the perception of oneness is not distinct.

The feeling that others are actually oneself is still weak.

True understanding can take place only when the aspect of oneness has been realized in depth.

Even after kensho, when you perceive that everything is one and are no longer confronted by an external world, you still cannot live in and through that experience.

Harada Roshi makes the same points, as does Kapleau in his introductions.

Despite all these caveats, the dominant chord of the book *is* a testimonial to the splendor of enlightenment. What is more, each account suggests a spiritual rebirth of life-altering significance. Now, readers

Standing by Enlightenment Without Resting in It

might expect a great master like Bassui to speak of his enlightenment in the most inspired terms, and also notable teachers like Yasutani Roshi and Harada Roshi (just to mention the principal protagonists of the book). But to hear one lay author after another, in the kensho accounts, describe his or her experience as deeply stirring or overwhelmingly joyous is to infer, willy-nilly, that such reactions are typical. However, I have found, in working with students, that reactions to a first opening are usually not that dramatic.

Most of the kensho accounts in *The Three Pillars* are presented in terms of passing one's first koan, usually Mu. But the truth is that this initial insight, even when accompanied by rapture, in and of itself seldom has a significant and lasting effect on the person. In fact, passing a first koan like Mu often means little more than that the student has had just enough insight into the nondual nature of reality that he or she can work effectively on subsequent koans. It is probably this level of insight that "Student J" equates with enlightenment when she says to Yasutani Roshi, in dokusan: "I have lived with people who have had an enlightenment experience, yet instead of becoming less grasping and selfish and egotistical, they sometimes become more so." In reply, Yasutani Roshi again states that "with a first enlightenment the realization of oneness is usually shallow." He then adds, "One whose actions are still dominated by ego cannot be said to have had a valid enlightenment." Fair enough, but that still leaves a wide range of insight — and ambiguity — between being "dominated by ego" and the selflessness of true enlightenment in the classic sense.

Although the kensho accounts in *The Three Pillars* are all included as "enlightenment experiences," we are given to know that they are not all deep. In the third, Yasutani Roshi warns the "Japanese garden designer" how tentative his opening is: "You have only caught a glimpse of the realm 'beyond the manifestation of form.' Your kensho is such that you can easily lose sight of it if you become lazy and foergo further practice." And further: "Right now you do not, so to speak, 'own' your realization." In the fourth, the "Japanese retired government worker" comments, after being passed by Yasutani Roshi on Mu:

A full kensho-awakening usually generates not only astonishment but also profound joy, but I neither wept nor laughed with joy. In most cases it transforms one's fundamental outlook on life and death and offers a new and penetrating insight into the words "Life is vain and

KJOLHEDE

transitory." But my experience carried in its wake no such insights, for it was but a touch of enlightenment.

The other experiences, however, are described as deeply affecting, and are accompanied by joy, bliss, and peace. Are we to conclude, then, that they were deeper?

Not necessarily. In his introduction to the dokusan section, Kapleau relates an anecdote told to him by Yasutani Roshi about a man who had had a kensho ("admittedly shallow") but failed to recognize it as such because it came without an emotional upheaval. "The nature of the reaction to one's enlightenment," Kapleau adds, "depends not only on the depth of the enlightenment itself but also on one's emotional and mental make-up."

Were the eight authors of the more dramatic accounts more emotional, or more deeply awakened, or some combination of the two? There is a third factor to be considered, as Kapleau points out in his introduction to the accounts: "All were written soon after the experience with the exception of number three, which was not set to paper until almost twenty years later." Nine of the stories, then, end with the kensho itself or at a point no more than several weeks after the kensho, and reflect no later perspective. Readers who are new to Zen, unfamiliar with the terrain of more advanced spiritual practice, are not likely to have questions about what happened later. Most of them probably thrill to the "success" of the authors. Readers with years of zazen under their belts, however, may be left wondering how those "winners" fared in the years following their experiences. The first two, we know, went on to become distinguished teachers of Zen. Have the others continued in Zen practice? If not, why not? How smoothly have their experiences borne them along through life's inevitable vicissitudes?

Kensho is not a Zen version of going to heaven. An awakened person may have her head in the clouds, but where else could her feet be but on the ground? And in this earthly world of form and phenomena, a first kensho still leaves plenty of debris to clean up. If before awakening you have a particular problem with fear, for example, afterward it will revisit you, like the Ghost of Christmas Past. The strength of the problem will have diminished in accordance with the depth of the opening, but there it will be. The same will be true with, say, depression, impatience, sexual cravings, jealousy, arrogance, and any of 1,001 other residual body-mind tendencies. Harada Roshi, at an advanced age, told Kapleau that as a young man, before beginning Zen practice, he had had a terri-

Standing by Enlightenment Without Resting in It

ble temper, and that after his kensho it took him another ten years of monastic training before he felt free of it.

Enlightenment in the classic sense, as the ancient masters used the word, is exceedingly rare, especially as a first opening. Those old masters knew, through their own experience, that even full-bodied awakening does not eradicate ego. The great Chinese Zen master Kuei-shan instructed:

> If a man is truly enlightened and has realized the fundamental . . . he is no longer tied to the poles of cultivation and noncultivation. But ordinarily, even though the mind has been awakened by an intervening cause . . . there still remains the inertia of habit, formed since the beginning of time, which cannot be eliminated at a stroke. He must be taught to cut off completely the stream of his habitual ideas and views caused by the still-operative karmas.[3]

Just what good, then, is a first kensho? If it is indeed genuine, it reveals the insubstantiality of all phenomena, so that neither thoughts nor the so-called outside world can ever deceive you again in the same way. It confirms that there is nothing outside your own mind, an insight which fundamentally changes your relationship to people, to things, and to change itself. And it reveals the bedrock of faith: that there is only this enlightened Self-nature. Although lingering emotional afflictions and other habitual tendencies will maintain a presence, you will be quicker to notice them as they arise, and, recognizing them as the flickering shadows that they are, you will be less likely to be drawn in by them. They become less and less of a problem. In general, pain and struggle remain as conditions of life, but your relationship to them will have changed, rendering them lighter and easier to manage.

The kensho accounts in *The Three Pillars* leave even seasoned Zen practitioners wondering about the nitty-gritty of daily life for those authors in the months and years that followed their openings. We do get one retrospective in *The Three Pillars* itself, from the Japanese garden designer, as mentioned above. We hear another in Roshi Kapleau's later *Zen: Merging of East and West*, which includes much material disabusing readers of romantic notions about the impact of kensho. In that book, a participant at an introductory workshop on Zen asks Roshi Kapleau, "Doesn't enlightenment clear away imperfections and personality flaws?" His reply: "No, it shows them up!"[4] This answer echoes the Chinese monk Tung-shan Liang-chieh, who was asked immediately after his awakening, "Are you happy now?" Tung-shan replied, "It's not that I'm not happy, but my happiness is like that of someone who has picked up a bright pearl from a heap of garbage."[5] My own experiences, as well as reports I have heard from others, match Tung-shan's sentiments: one does not remain long at the emotional heights described in *The Three Pillars*. In fact, years later you wonder how you could have imagined that it was any kind of crowning experience.

By far the most significant vista revealed by kensho is the vastness of Mind and the great distance one still has to go to approach full realization. Zen master Dogen warned:

> You only get it when you're still halfway.
> If you find that you've gone all the way, keep going.

The deeper the awakening, the more conspicuous become the lingering impurities, which come to appear ever more subtle and textured. It is like climbing a mountain and at every plateau seeing layered hills that recede further into the hazy distance. To be afforded such a view might be intolerably daunting if one had not also seen that those body-mind defilements are essentially empty, devoid of any self-substance. With continued practice, the impurities evoke less aversion and more fascination at their staying power.

The enlightenment section of *The Three Pillars* may leave readers with romantic notions of kensho as a climactic achievement, but the Iwasaki letters in the following section provide a vaster perspective. Yaeko Iwasaki was a young Japanese woman, in fragile health most of her life, who died of tuberculosis in 1935. In just the last few days before her death, she had a series of successively deeper awakenings, as confirmed by Harada Roshi. These letters are stirring testimony to the spirit of ceaseless exertion. Who could not marvel at Yaeko's faith and courage, at the determination that braced her efforts? To those who have passed the first gate — or the second, or third — she is an awe-inspiring model. A Chinese Zen master could have had her in mind when he said, "The unenlightened must strive as if mourning father and mother. The enlightened, too, must strive as if mourning father and mother."

Psychological research has shown that the greater the emphasis placed on a certain goal, the greater the likelihood that people will stop after attaining that goal. In my teaching I no longer speak of kensho as anything to set one's sights on; nor do I inflate expectations associated with passing one's first koan. Too many students have managed to break through this

Standing by Enlightenment Without Resting in It

first barrier only to find that it was hardly the silver bullet they had imagined it would be. A person with "the mind that seeks the Way" will shrug
off this element of morning-after disappointment and persevere, but a less
experienced student with just a faint opening may lose faith in the practice. In consideration of this, I have grown increasingly strict about passing people on their first koan. At the same time, I have tried to raise the
bar by speaking more consistently of *deep* awakening, or even *full* awakening, which is a goal we can all work toward together.

Given that even a solid kensho is but the entrance to the true
Dharma, and that *The Three Pillars of Zen* reminds us of this repeatedly, why are so many practitioners so eager to clutch at kensho as the be-
all and end-all? Why are we so ready to be borne aloft, on wings of
desire, by tales of heroic spiritual struggle and the promise of a fabled
Lotus Land of enlightenment? Because we know they are not mere
tales, and that right where we stand is indeed the true Lotus Land. At
some level of the mind we know that enlightenment is our nature. We
resonate to first-hand accounts of awakening because we recognize
Home when we hear about it. Damn the torpedoes—full speed ahead!

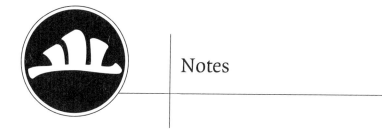

Notes

Introduction

1. A new edition of *The Three Pillars of Zen* is forthcoming from Doubleday in 2000.

2. The most recent editions of Kapleau's other books are: *The Zen of Living and Dying: A Practical and Spiritual Guide* (Boston: Shambhala, 1998); *Awakening to Zen: The Teachings of Roshi Philip Kapleau*, Polly Young-Eisendrath and Rafe Martin, eds. (New York: Scribner, 1997); *Zen: Merging of East and West* (Garden City, N. Y.: Anchor Press/Doubleday, 1989); and *To Cherish All Life: A Buddhist View of Animal Slaughter and Meat Eating* (Rochester, N. Y.: Rochester Zen Center, 1981).

3. Kapleau's sanctioned Dharma heirs are Mitra Bishop, Zenson Gifford, Sunyana Graef, Danan Henry, Bodhin Kjolhede, Sunya Kjolhede, and Lawson Sachter.

4. *American Zen Twenty Years* (Rochester, N.Y.: Rochester Zen Center, 1986), 7. Kapleau's most detailed autobiographical account is found in *Zen: Merging of East and West*, 259–70.

5. This statement is a generalization. In some schools, including most of contemporary Soto Zen, certification to teach is not framed in terms of spiritual attainment.

6. Joan Baez, "Merton the Prophet," in Paul Wilkes, ed., *Merton By Those Who Knew Him Best* (San Francisco: Harper & Row, 1984), 43.

7. Ken Wilber, *Eye to Eye: The Quest for the New Paradigm* (Garden City, N.Y.: Anchor Press/Doubleday, 1983), 264.

8. Kapleau, *Zen: Merging of East and West*, 259.

9. Winston Davis is credited with the phrase "rapid upward spiritual mobility."

10. Robert Coles, *The Secular Mind* (Princeton: Princeton University Press, 1999), 32.

11. Kenneth Kraft, *Eloquent Zen: Daito and Early Japanese Zen* (Honolulu: University of Hawaii Press, 1992), 89.

12. Bernard Faure, *The Rhetoric of Immediacy: A Cultural Critique of Chan/Zen Buddhism* (Princeton: Princeton University Press, 1991; John R. McRae, "The Story of Early Ch'an," in Kenneth Kraft, ed., *Zen: Tradition and Transition* (New York: Grove Press, 1988), 137. The nuanced views of both Faure and McRae on the relation between Zen experience and Zen language are not reducible to the phrases cited here.

13. Robert H. Sharf, "The Zen of Japanese Nationalism," in Donald S. Lopez, Jr., ed., *Curators of the Buddha: The Study of Buddhism under Colonialism* (Chicago: University of Chicago Press, 1995), 108.

14. Philip Kapleau, "The Private Encounter with the Master," in Kraft, *Zen: Tradition and Transition*, 51.

15. Kapleau, Zen: *Merging of East and West*, 294, 296–97.

Notes

16. Thomas Merton, *Conjectures of a Guilty Bystander*, cited in Wilkes, *Merton By Those Who Knew Him Best*, 95.

17. Joseph Mitsuo Kitagawa, "Buddhism in the Modern World," in Jaroslav Pelikan, ed., *The World Treasury of Modern Religious Thought* (Boston: Little, Brown, 1990), 360; reprinted from a work originally published in 1960.

18. Rochester Zen Center, "Leaves in the Wind: The Memories of Roshi Philip Kapleau" (video, 1998).

19. Robert Sharf uses the phrase "democratization of enlightenment" (with quotation marks) in connection with Sanbokyodan, the religious organization founded by Yasutani Hakuun. See Robert H. Sharf, "Sanbokyodan: Zen and the Way of the New Religions," in *Japanese Journal of Religious Studies* 22:3–4 (1995), 437.

20. Carl Bode, ed., *The Portable Thoreau* (New York: Viking Press, 1964), 360.

⚓︎

What's the Difference between a Buddhist and a Non-Buddhist?

1. D. T. Suzuki, *The Training of the Zen Monk* (New York: University Books, 1965), 97.

2. Ironically, it was Roshi Kapleau who introduced me to Saint Anthony.

3. Philip Kapleau, *The Zen of Living and Dying* (Boston: Shambala, 1998), 30.

4. J. Hardon, S.J., *The Catholic Catechism* (New York: Doubleday, 1981), 37.

5. Dwight Goddard, *A Buddhist Bible* (Boston: Beacon Press, 1966), 4.

6. Hardon, *The Catholic Catechism*, 69, 80.

7. Philip Kapleau, *Zen: Merging of East and West* (Garden City, N.Y.: Anchor Press/Doubleday, 1989), 265.

8. The Dalai Lama, *Kindness, Clarity, and Insight* (Ithaca, N.Y.: Snow Lion, 1988), 49.

♨

The Authoritative Gaze

1. Morinaga Soko, "My Struggle to Become a Zen Monk," in Kenneth Kraft, ed., *Zen: Tradition and Transition* (New York: Grove Press, 1988), 16.

2. Ibid., 16.

3. Czeslaw Milosz, *The Separate Notebooks* (Hopewell, N.J.: Ecco Press, 1984), 145.

4. Katherine Pratt Ewing, *Arguing Sainthood: Modernity, Psychoanalysis, and Islam* (Durham, N.C.: Duke University Press, 1997), 262.

5. William Shakespeare, *Macbeth*, act I, scene 3.

6. Ramana Maharshi, *The Spiritual Teaching of Ramana Maharshi* (Boston: Shambhala, 1988), 66.

♨

Many Paths, One Path

1. Kazuaki Tanahashi, ed., *Moon in a Dewdrop: Writings of Zen Master Dogen* (San Francisco: North Point Press, 1985), 30.

♨

Seeing the Ox: A Second Look

1. Susan Murcott, *The First Buddhist Women: Translations and Commentary on the Therigatha* (Berkeley: Parallax Press, 1991), 48, 27, 34.

2. Master Daibi of Unkan, in Yoko Okuda, trans., Torei Enji, *The Discourse on the Inexhuastible Lamp of the Zen School* (Rutland, Vt.: Charles E. Tuttle Co., 1996), 182.

3. Ibid., 177.

Notes

Standing by Enlightenment Without Resting in It

1. Yoko Okuda, trans., Torei Enji, *The Discourse on the Inexhaustible Lamp of the Zen School* (Rutland, Vt.: Charles Tuttle Co., 1996), 74.

2. Robert H. Sharf, "Sanbokyodan: Zen and the Way of the New Religions," in *Japanese Journal of Religious Studies* 22: 3–4 (1995), 429–30.

3. John C. H. Wu, *The Golden Age of Zen*, rev. ed. (New York: Doubleday, 1996), 112–13.

4. Philip Kapleau, *Zen: Merging of East and West* (Garden City, N. Y.: Anchor Press/Doubleday, 1989), 31.

5. Wu, *The Golden Age of Zen*, 131.

Contributors

MITRA BISHOP, a sanctioned heir of Roshi Philip Kapleau, spent several years training in a Japanese temple. She is the resident teacher at Mountain Gate temple near Santa Fe.

WES BORDEN, professor of chemistry at the University of Washington at Seattle, was a long-time student of Roshi Kapleau. Since Roshi Kapleau's retirement, he has trained with Harada Shodo Roshi.

CASEY FRANK, a senior disciple of Roshi Kapleau, currently works in Denver as an attorney and an educator.

SUNYANA GRAEF, a sanctioned heir of Roshi Kapleau, has been the teacher at the Vermont Zen Center since 1988. She also is the teacher of the Toronto and Costa Rica Zen Centers.

VICTORIA KIEBURTZ is a physician and a member of the board of trustees of the Rochester Zen Center.

BODHIN KJOLHEDE was appointed Roshi Kapleau's successor at the Rochester Zen Center in 1986. He will inaugurate the Chapin Mill Retreat Center in 2000.

ARNOLD KOTLER is editor-in-chief of Parallax Press and cofounder of the Community of Mindful Living, based in Berkeley. He is a sanctioned heir of Thich Nhat Hanh and a former student of Roshis Shunryu Suzuki and Richard Baker.

KENNETH KRAFT is chair of the department of Religious Studies at Lehigh University in Bethlehem, Pennsylvania. He is the author of *Eloquent Zen* and *The Wheel of Engaged Buddhism*, and the editor of several books on contemporary Buddhism.

RAFE MARTIN is a professional storyteller and author of award-winning children's books. In 1997 he coedited Roshi Kapleau's book *Awakening to Zen*. He lives in Rochester, New York.

JOSH SCHREI has spent the past three years organizing concerts around the world on behalf of the Tibetan freedom movement. He grew up at the Rochester Zen Center, where his parents served on the resident staff.

ALAN SENAUKE is a resident priest at the Berkeley Zen Center and director of the Buddhist Peace Fellowship. He is a sanctioned heir of Sojun Mel Weitsman.

ALBERT STUNKARD is professor of psychiatry and former chair of the department at the University of Pennsylvania School of Medicine. He was D. T. Suzuki's physician during the American occupation of Japan.

The "weathermark" identifies this book as a production of Weatherhill, Inc., publishers of fine books on Asia and the Pacific. Editorial Supervision: Jeffrey Hunter. Book and cover design: Noble & Israel Design. Production Supervision: Bill Rose. Printing and binding: R. R. Donnelly. The typeface used is Electra, with Quadraat for display.